Motorbooks International Illustrated Buyer's Guide Series

Illustrated

Thunderbird

BUYER'S ★ GUIDE

D1710485

Paul G. McLaughlin

Motorbooks International
Publishers & Wholesalers

*This book is dedicated to the memory of my uncle Francis P. McLaughlin,
who was a great inspiration to me. During the course of his life, my Uncle Fran had quite a few cars,
including some rather neat-looking Thunderbirds. One of the classiest cars that I remember him owning was
a beautiful Royal Burgundy 1960 Thunderbird hardtop. As far as I am concerned, that was one of the
sharpest-looking Thunderbirds I have ever seen. Though my Uncle Fran has died, his memory will live on
for me every time I see or think about a Royal Burgundy 1960 Thunderbird hardtop.*

First published in 1994 by Motorbooks International Publishers & Wholesalers, PO Box 2, 729 Prospect Avenue, Osceola, WI 54020 USA

© Paul G. McLaughlin, 1994

Motorbooks International books are also available at discounts in bulk quantity for industrial or sales-promotional use. For details write to Special Sales Manager at the Publisher's address

Library of Congress Cataloging-in-Publication Data

McLaughlin, Paul G.
    Illustrated Thunderbird buyer's guide/Paul G. McLaughlin.
        p. cm. — (Motorbooks International illustrated buyer's guide series)
        Includes index.
        ISBN 0-87938-870-6
        1. Thunderbird automobile—Purchasing.
    2. Thunderbird automobile—History. I. Title.
    II. Series.
    TL215.T46M38 1994
    629.222′2—dc20   94-1460

On the front cover: For those who liked their muscle wrapped in a bit of luxury, Ford offered the 1963 390ci 3x2bbl M-code Thunderbird. This arresting red example belongs to Bill and Barbara Jacobsen of Silver Dollar Classics in Odessa, FL. *Mike Mueller*

On the back cover: All photos courtesy of Ford Public Relations.

Printed and bound in the United States of America

Contents

Acknowledgments

I would like to thank the following individuals for their help in preparing this book. Their efforts on my behalf are truly appreciated.
Paul McLaughlin, Sr., Arlington, MA; Robert Lucero, D.D.S., Albuquerque, NM;
C. Gayle Warnock, Scottsdale, AZ; Ken Campbell, Albuquerque, NM; John McLaughlin, Arlington, MA; George Hinds, Cambridge, MA; Alan Clarke, Arlington, MA; Dick Copello, York, PA; Danny and Melissa Deaver, Albuquerque, NM; Melissa Deaver, Albuquerque, NM; Ford Motor Company, Dearborn, MI; Ford Photographic, Dearborn, MI; Ford Motor Company Public Affairs, Dearborn, MI; Bernice McLaughlin, Albuquerque, NM; Jessica McLaughlin, Albuquerque, NM; Amy McLaughlin, Albuquerque, NM; Paul C. McLaughlin, Albuquerque, NM; Murray Wells, Marshall, TX; Allen Biggs, Boulder, CO; Jim Petrick, Madeira, OH; Elliott Kahn, Clearwater Beach, FL; Jerry Bougher, Albany, OR; Rod Kilvington, Northfield, South Australia; Pete Sessler, Milford, PA; Scott Logan, Richfield, MN; Randy Mason, Henry Ford Museum, Dearborn, MI; Archie Stutt, Hamilton, New Zealand; Graham Stevens, Sydney, Australia; Lois Eminger, Dearborn, MI.

Unless otherwise noted, photographs were taken by the author. Most illustrations came from Ford Motor Company materials and are used with permission.

Chapter 1

Pre-Thunderbird

To gain a better appreciation of the Thunderbird and its impact on buyers and the fortunes of the Ford Motor Company, it's best to return to the car's roots. Learning how these cars moved from concept to production will lend insight into the workings of a large automotive corporation back in the early-1950s. To understand the whys and the wherefores of the early Thunderbirds, one has to examine the automotive scene just after World War II.

Automotive development and production for the civilian market was put on hold during the war, so manufacturers didn't real-ly have anything new to offer their customers immediately after the war ended. Fortunately, pent-up demand for anything automotive kept the assembly lines moving and the cash coming in during the immediate postwar period. Still, manufacturers realized that this seller's market wouldn't last indefinitely. They knew they would have to devise some exciting new product to appeal to a market that was becoming ever more selective and sophisticated.

Soldiers returning from Europe and Asia comprised a large portion of this burgeoning market. While stationed abroad, American

This prototype promotional Thunderbird photograph shows the subject in a suburban setting. Note the 1955 Fairlane side trim. *Ford Motor Company*

5

The 1955 Fairlane Crown Victoria hardtop was Ford's top-of-the-line full-size car. The Fairlane's "check" trim was once considered for installation on the Thunderbird, too.

GIs came into contact with cars that were smaller, sportier, and more fun to drive than the vehicles they had grown up with in the United States. Cars like the MG TC, Jaguar, and Mercedes Benz were very popular among GIs, and that popularity didn't go unnoticed by U.S. auto manufacturers, especially when customers began asking why they couldn't have American cars with the same attributes. U.S. manufacturers even went so far as to send representatives to European car shows to investigate what sort of designs the foreign competition was working on—with an eye toward incorporating some of that foreign flair into their own products.

One of those representatives was a man by the name of Lewis D. Crusoe, a Ford vice-president and general manager whom Henry Ford II had selected to help turn around Ford Motor Company. In the late-1940s, Ford Motor Company was struggling from a myriad of problems, leading Henry to seek out Crusoe to provide some inspiration and direction to his floundering company. Crusoe was a good automotive man with a keen sense of what would sell in the American marketplace. And, thanks to his position within the company, he wielded considerable power and prestige, usually getting what he wanted.

Crusoe went to Europe on a fairly regular basis, where he liked to make the rounds of all the auto shows. His favorite was the annual Paris Auto Show, which typically attracted the cream of the automotive crop. It was in

The 1955 Thunderbird in this promotional photograph is wearing 1955 Fairlane headlight covers rather than the more plain Thunderbird style. *Ford Motor Company*

This prototype, early-model Thunderbird is wearing a set of 1954 Ford deluxe, full-size wheel covers. *Ford Motor Company*

Paris in 1951 or 1952 that Crusoe decided that Ford needed a small, sporty car of its own—a car that would add a little excitement and prestige to the line. Unbeknownst to Crusoe at the time, a small cadre of Ford employees were already at work on a sports car project, albeit unofficially. With Crusoe's blessing and support, the project really started to take off. Crusoe's only stipulations were that the car look like a Ford and that it bring some prestige to the Ford Motor Company.

Because of the backing he lent the project, most people credit Lewis Crusoe with being the "Father of the Thunderbird." This project, however, was not a one-man show by any stretch of the imagination. Many talented people were drawn into the project from its conception to completion, including. Frank Q.

A profile shot like this highlights the 1955 Thunderbird's timeless styling features. The long front end and short rear deck were features that returned to the Ford lineup in the 1960s with the release of the Mustang.

Hershey, Ford's chief stylist during most of the Thunderbird project's early days; stylists and designers Gene Bordinat, Damon Woods, Bill Boyer, George Walker, Joe Oros, Bob Maguire, Charles Waterhouse, and Elwood Engel; project planner Thomas B. Case; and chief engineer Bill Burnett.

While the Thunderbird Project was materializing at Ford, a similar project was underway at Chevrolet. The Corvette was also penned as a two-seat sports car, but this is where the similarities between the two projects ended. The Thunderbird would look like a scaled-down Ford, whereas the Corvette didn't look anything like any Chevrolet then in production. The Thunderbird would use a steel body, while the Corvette would use a body made out fiberglass—a new material for automotive use at that time. The Thunderbird would use a V-8 engine backed by a choice of automatic or standard transmissions, while the Corvette would offer only a souped-up six-cylinder engine connected to an automatic transmission. Thunderbird buyers would also have their choice of several exterior colors, whereas the Corvette was available in white only.

With less to offer and less to worry about, the Corvette beat the Thunderbird to market by a full year. It briefly basked in the limelight, but once the Thunderbird hit the streets, the Corvette quickly fell from grace—a plummeting so severe that Chevrolet considered dropping the Corvette. Ultimately, Chevrolet realized this was one market segment it simply couldn't afford to abandon; it needed a car with which to compete with Ford for those buyers looking for something a little sporty and distinctive from an American manufacturer.

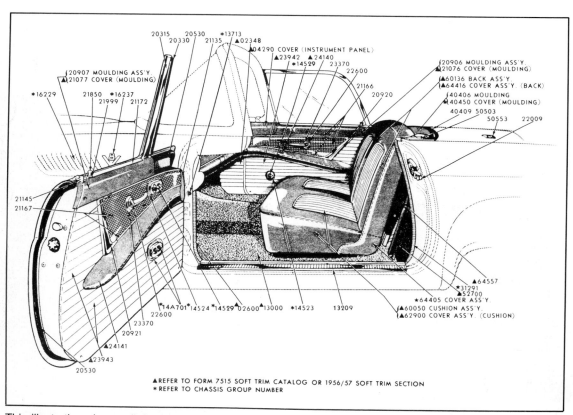

This illustration shows all the interior details of the 1955–1957 Thunderbirds. *Ford Motor Company*

★★★	1955 Thunderbird
★★★	1956 Thunderbird
★★★★	1956 "E" Thunderbird
★★★★	1957 Thunderbird
★★★★	1957 "E" Thunderbird
★★★★★	1957 "F" Thunderbird

1955-1957: The Birth of a Cult Classic

For people who appreciate fine automobiles, February 20, 1954, will go down in the annals of automobiledom as a truly milestone day. It was on this day at the Detroit Auto Show that the public first laid eyes on Ford's new Thunderbird.

The car shown at Detroit and other similar shows over the next few months was a prototype of a vehicle that was to join the Ford lineup in the fall of 1954 as a new 1955 model. Visitors to the show let Ford know that they were impressed with this new car and could not wait to get their hands on one.

Some of those people on hand for the premiere showing were reporters for national magazines and newspapers, and their glowing reports appeared in *Time*, *Newsweek*, *Sports Illustrated*, *Popular Science*, and other publications. The spell had been cast, and now it was up to Ford to deliver these cars to their dealers.

A rear view of the 1955 Thunderbird. Note "NIFTY-5" license plate. This car, reported to be the twenty-ninth built, belongs to Bob Inskeep of Farmington, N.M.

The gasoline door on 1955 Thunderbirds carried the Ford crest and crossed flags emblem.

Here is a tastefully modified 1955 Thunderbird. Non-stock items include a vintage, custom tube grille and vintage Halibrand racing wheels.

Early-model 1955 Thunderbird on display beside a 1957 model and a 1955 Fairlane Crown Victoria. *Ford Motor Company*

1955

Thunderbird production started on September 9, 1954, in Ford's Dearborn Assembly Plant in the River Rouge Complex. The first Thunderbirds were soon trucked out to dealerships from coast to coast. These early Thunderbirds were built on the same assembly line as regular Fords, so it took some time to manufacture enough of them to meet demand.

You know this has to be an early Thunderbird advertisement because only a very few early-1955 Thunderbirds wore the 1955 Fairlane side trim.

The official introductory date for the new Thunderbird was October 22, 1954. On that day, Ford dealerships across the country were besieged by people trying to get a close-up look at the new car. Dealers took about 4,000 orders for the Thunderbird on that first day—a remarkable feat for such a new car at that time. It took Ford almost three months to produce that many Thunderbirds, so waiting lists were fairly common.

The Thunderbird was designed to be a smaller and sportier version of the regular, full-sized Ford. And it hit that mark squarely on the head. Unlike the Corvette and regular Chevrolet, there was a strong family resemblance between the Ford and the Thunderbird. The Thunderbird used many regular Ford parts, including wheel covers, taillights, interior pieces, engines, transmissions, and other mechanical parts. There was even a time, albeit a short one, when thought was given to using the new Fairlane "side spear" trim on the Thunderbird. Early advertisements and photographs for the 1955 Thunderbird showed this trim installed. There were even a few cars that came from the factory this way. It has been reported that Lewis Cru-

A restored 1955 Thunderbird in top-down form at an eastern car show in 1992.

soe's personal 1955 Thunderbird wore this trim. The Fairlane trim looked nice on the Fairlane, but on the Thunderbird, it looked out of place. Thankfully it was left off the regular production Thunderbirds.

These new Thunderbirds featured bodies supplied to Ford by the Budd Automotive Company. Budd stamped out the body panels and welded them into a beautiful "body in

Another shot of a 1955 Thunderbird wearing 1955 Fairlane trim. This car also features wire wheel covers and an aftermarket Continental Kit. When this photograph was taken, this car belonged to Lewis D. Crusoe. *Ford Motor Company*

hardtop. Base price was around $2,900. It's not likely that many Thunderbirds left Ford in base trim, however. Most came equipped with a convertible top, automatic transmission, power brakes, power steering, fender skirts, power seats, and a radio—boosting the price to $4,000, which still wasn't too bad of a price for a limited-production, prestigious, sporty automobile. To keep up with demand, the 1955 Ford Thunderbird was in production for almost a full year. In that time Ford produced and sold 16,155 Thunderbirds.

1956

The 1955 Thunderbird had a lot going for it, but there were some minor problems that generated customer complaints. Ford addressed these issues for 1956. One problem the 1955s had was too much heat in the floor area. This heat was drawn into the cockpit from the lower firewall area and the transmission tunnel. To help alleviate the problem,

white" that was then trucked over to the Ford plant, where they were painted and trimmed out. The body was then matched to a chassis on the regular assembly line. Quality control was of utmost concern, and everyone involved in the project strove to make these cars as good as they could be.

For a 1955 automobile, the standard Thunderbird came pretty well equipped, including a 292ci Thunderbird V-8, a three-speed manual transmission with floor shift, an adjustable steering column, an electric clock, a tachometer, and a fiberglass bolt-on

Check out the "Dagmars" mounted on this Thunderbird's bumper guards. This car also features unique hood and fender ornaments, two-tone paint, special side trim, and the Thunderbird engine emblem as used on the 1956 Fairlane.

Although this ad is wrinkled now, it is a good one to have in a Thunderbird paper collection because it shows the 1956 car with top-down, convertible top-up, and hardtop installed. *Jerry Bougher Ads*

Murray Wells, from Marshall, Texas, is an early Thunderbird enthusiast. He has had quite a few of these desirable 'Birds over the years, including this beautiful red 1955 that now sits in his garage. *Murray Wells Collection*

Ford added adjustable air vent doors to the 1956's front fenders, providing flow-through ventilation. This cooled the floorboards but didn't entirely eliminate the heat problem.

Another problem from 1955 involved transmission overheating. To better cool the gearbox, 1956 Thunderbirds had cooling lines running from the Fordomatic transmission forward to the radiator, where incoming air helped dissipate some of the heat generated in the transmission.

Another complaint logged by 1955 Thunderbird buyers concerned wind buffeting in the passenger compartment. Ford solved this problem by going back to a design of the 1930s: the practice of using windwings to help deflect air flowing in and around the passenger compartment.

The smallish trunk of 1955 Thunderbirds was filled mostly with spare tire, leaving room to carry little else. To cure this problem for 1956, Ford moved the spare tire out of the trunk and into a continental spare tire carrier attached to the bumper. Although this arrangement solved one problem, it created another, adding about 10in to the Thunderbird's length. Positioning the additional weight of the tire and carrier so far from the

This 1957 Thunderbird proposal features a unique front bumper, front wheel cove sculpturing, and different rear wheel cutout. Note the unusual top treatment with its special window. Also note that bumper trim, parking lights, and headlight doors differ on each side of the car.

This pre-prototype 1956 Thunderbird photograph shows a car wearing a special hardtop. The hardtop had a window installed to help cut down on its blind spot. *Ford Motor Company*

This sharp-looking, restored 1956 Thunderbird awaits its turn on the auction block in 1992. Early-model Thunderbirds are very popular and always receive much attention at auctions.

rear axle also created handling problems. To some people, this trade-off was acceptable; all they had to do was change their driving habits.

These were the major changes that Ford made to the 1956 Thunderbird, but they weren't the only ones. Under the hood, Ford punched out the 292ci Y-block to 312ci, thus creating an engine it called the Thunderbird Special V-8. It was available as an option to the 292 and could be mated with either Fordomatic or overdrive transmissions. Horse-

power ratings for this 312 were 215 with an overdrive transmission and 225 with a Fordomatic. Cars fitted with the conventional three-speed manual transmission could only be had with 292 engines, according to literature of the time. With a horsepower rating of 202, these three-speed Thunderbirds were no slouches by any stretch of the imagination. Later in the year, Ford offered a "dual-quad" (2x4bbl) carburetor and intake manifold op-

Rear three-quarters view of this 1956 Thunderbird shows a Continental Kit and redesigned rear bumper. Carrying the spare tire in a Continental Kit provided some extra room in the Thunderbird's smallish trunk. *Ford Motor Company*

"Even dreamier-even newer" magazine advertisement appeared in March 1956. It shows a Thunderbird at a sporting event and with a street scene in the background. *Jerry Bougher Ads*

"A Mink Coat for Father" was a clever way to market Thunderbirds to men back in 1956. *Jerry Bougher Ads*

This 1956 Thunderbird's restored engine compartment shows its "see clear" windshield washer bag, unique air cleaner box, and cast-aluminum, finned valve covers.

tion for the 312. This optional engine was rated at 260hp, which, in a car weighing only about 3,000lb, made for some pretty exciting driving.

Ford changed the electrical system in all its cars for 1956, going from a 6-volt to 12-volt set-up. This necessitated changing all electrical components, starters, switches, relays, voltage regulators, instruments, lights, etc.

Interior updates were also made for 1956. For safety purposes, Ford went to a deep dish-design steering wheel and revised the dashboard to increase its effectiveness in preventing injuries to the driver and passenger. Ford also made changes in the trimming on the seat and door panels.

Another problem area on the early Thunderbirds involved the large blind spot found on the car's right-hand side and caused by the roof's wide "C" panel. Ford designers tried all sorts of window treatments that would allow more light into the car. Ultimately, the design selected was one of circular windows and trim not unlike the portholes of a ship. In fact, that ship resemblance is how this type of window got its "porthole" name. The addition of these windows both provided the driver with a better view of the right-hand side of the car and let more light into the cockpit, making it look more airy and brighter. As an added bonus, these windows made the roof

and the whole car look more stylish. However, if a buyer preferred the look of the old roof, Ford still offered it, too.

Ford also changed the design of the 1956 Thunderbird's rear bumper, moving the exhaust outlets from the center pod location of 1955 to the sides of the bumpers. Changes were also made in exterior trim, taillights, and headlamp doors.

Although most of these changes improved the Thunderbird, they didn't help Ford post better sales: 15,631 Thunderbirds were built and sold in model year 1956, down slightly from 1955.

1957

With all its improvements, the 1956 Thunderbird was a pretty tough act to follow. But Ford was more than up to the task, as they proved in September 1956, when the new 1957 Thunderbirds debuted.

The 1957 Thunderbird featured the first major restyling done to the original Thunderbird body. Starting at the front, Ford changed the bumper and grille, as well as the front fenders. Moving back along the body, Ford redesigned the doors and quarter panels adding some modest fins at the rear. These fins were rather tame compared to others of the time. Ford also widened and extended the trunk an additional 6in enabling the spare tire to fit inside it while still providing enough room for other incidentals. Moving the spare tire back inside the trunk allowed Ford to scrap the continental kit and restyle the back bumper and taillights.

Another change Ford incorporated in the 1957 Thunderbird involved its wheels and tires. The earlier cars had run on 15in wheels and tires, but the new Thunderbirds rode on 14-inchers. The smaller tires dropped the Thunderbird closer to the ground lending it a sleeker look.

Ford once again offered Thunderbird customers three tops from which to choose: a plain hardtop with no side windows, the porthole top, or a convertible top in rayon or vinyl. Rayon tops were available in black, blue, or tan, while the vinyl top was available only in white.

Interior changes for 1957 weren't as extensive as the exterior changes, consisting of

---

1956
Exterior Colors and Codes

Peacock Blue	(L)
Torch Red	(R)
Fiesta Red	(K)
Sunset Coral	(Y)
Colonial White	(E)
Buckskin Tan	(J)
Black	(A)
Goldenglow Yellow	(M)
Thunderbird Gray	(P)
Thunderbird Green	(Z)

Options

Lifeguard seat belts	SelectAire air conditioner
Windshield washers	Power steering
Power brakes	Power windows
Overdrive transmission	Fordomatic transmission
Fender skirts	Signal-seeking transistor radio
Whitewall tires	Thunderbird Special 312 V-8 engine

A little sticker placed on the windshield of this 1957 Thunderbird look-alike states that this particular car was "Proposal #3." Note the chrome on the rear fins and the lower rear quarter panel trim.

A close-up view of a 1957 Thunderbird instrument panel and steering wheel. Also note the radio, hang-on air conditioner, and gearshift lever. *Murray Wells Collection*

Now here's a unique-looking 1957 Thunderbird. Note the two-tone paint scheme, finned front fender trim, upper body chrome trim, and rear quarter panel accent trim.

new designs for the seat coverings and door panels and the instrument cluster.

Ford also made changes under the Thunderbird's hood by increasing the number of 312ci engines offered. Once again, the base engine and transmission was the 292 V-8 with three-speed manual system. This 292 Y-block came with a Holley 2-barrel carburetor atop a 2-barrel intake manifold and was rated at 212hp. Next in line was the Thunderbird 312 Special V-8 with a Holley 4-barrel carburetor and a 9.7:1 compression ratio. This engine put

This early model Thunderbird engine compartment has been dressed up with a chrome-plated air cleaner lid and cast-aluminum, finned valve covers.

Top-up or top-down, the 1957 Thunderbirds are beautiful cars. Wouldn't you like to own this pair? *Ford Motor Company*

out 245hp and 332lb-ft of torque at 3200rpm. Next on the engine roster was the Thunderbird 312 Super V-8. This engine carried an "E" engine code, and cars with this engine were called "E Birds." The 312 Super V-8 featured twin Holley 4-barrel carburetors atop a dual-quad intake manifold. This hot little number was rated at 270hp and produced 336lb-ft of torque at 3400rpm. A 285hp racing version of this engine was available.

If the E Bird wasn't hot enough for you, Ford had another ace up its sleeve to appeal to performance buffs: the Thunderbird Super-charged V-8. Cars equipped with this rare powerplant were called "F Birds," again because their engine code used the letter "F." These engines featured a McCulloch single stage, variable ratio, centrifugal-type super-charger (Model VR-57), which blew air into a sealed box that encased a Holley 4-barrel carburetor. Set up for street use, this engine carried a 300hp rating, but with some super tuning it could easily make 340–360hp. It's unfortunate for Thunderbird enthusiasts today that in 1957 Ford could find only 211 buyers who

Thunderbird script and simulated vent trim as applied to the front fenders of 1957 Thunderbirds.

This shot shows how much room was available in the 1957 Thunderbird trunk, considerably more than in the 1955 or 1956 models. *Murray Wells Collection*

19

Another design proposal for the 1957 Thunderbird. Notice that the left front fender and headlight treatment are similar to that applied to the regular 1957 Ford line. Also note the upper door treatment and rear quarter panel design.

wanted this supercharged engine. That 211 figure translates to about one F Bird for every 100 non-supercharged Thunderbirds produced in 1957.

The first 1957 Thunderbirds were built in September 1956, and the last 1957 Thunderbird, reportedly an E model car, was built on December 13, 1957—a rather fitting end to the production run of these two-seater classics. Ford produced 21,380 cars for the 1957 model year. When this figure is added to the two previous model year productions, we find that Ford produced 53,166 first-generation two-seater Thunderbirds in a little more than three years. During that same period, the Thunderbird's chief competition, the Corvette, saw production of only 14,446. When you realize it took Chevrolet five model years to reach that much lower production

Interior shot from a 1957 Thunderbird.

1957
Exterior Colors and Codes

Starmist Blue (F)	Willow Green (J)
Raven Black (A)	Gunmetal Gray (N, then H
Colonial White (E)	after 9/57)
Robin's Egg Blue (L)	Flame Red (J)
Platinum (H)	Coral Sand (Z)
Bronze (Q)	Inca Gold (Y)
Dusk Rose (X)	

Sun Gold (G, replaces Inca Gold after 9/57)
Torch Red (R, replaces Flame Red after 9/57)
Seaspray Green (N, replaces Willow Green after 9/57)
Azure Blue (I, replaces Starmist Blue after 9/57)

Options

Power brakes	Power steering
Four-way power seat	Power windows
Tonneau cover	Seat belts
Windshield washers	Engine dress-up kit
MagicAire heater	Deluxe antennas
Fender skirts	Backup lights
Locking gas cap	Turbine wheel covers
Whitewall tires	Wire wheel covers
Fordomatic transmission	Overdrive transmission
Hooded mirror	Town and Country radio
Front fender antenna	Rear-mounted antenna
312ci engine	McCulloch VR-57 super
	charger

Here's one rear end design proposal for the 1957 Thunderbird that we're glad wasn't chosen for the production car. Did you notice the headrest nacelles?

number it's pretty easy to see which car was the most popular.

A Word About 1955–57 Ratings

As far as rankings go, demand and rarity dictate that the F model 1957 Thunderbird be the number one collectible for this period. The 1957 E model would come in second, with the 1956 E Thunderbirds knocking down the third spot. Up next would be any 1957 Thunderbird, followed by the 1955 version since it is the first model of the run. And following the 1955 would be the 1956 models.

A couple of 1957 Thunderbirds on display at the Fabulous Fords Forever show in California. Early-model Thunderbirds are very popular in California and several show up for this show every year.

Here's one way to get around the problem of not enough seat space in a 1957 Thunderbird. This modern-day rumble seat was a period aftermarket item called a "Bird's Nest."

Power seat solenoids, electric motor, and other associated power seat apparatus, as found in the 1957 Thunderbird. *Murray Wells Collection*

This beautiful, black 1957 Thunderbird features some later-model Kelsey-Hayes wire wheels that add a very distinctive look. *Murray Wells Collection*

Thunderbirds are popular the world over. This beautiful, red 1956 model sits in a parking lot in Sydney, Australia. *Graham Stevens*

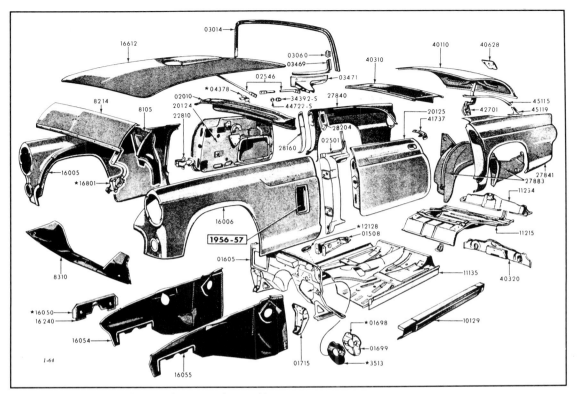

An exploded drawing of the various panels used in
early-model Thunderbirds. *Ford Motor Company*

Chapter 3

1958-1960: The Squarebirds Prove Bigger Is Really Better

★★★★★ 1958 Thunderbird Convertible
★★★★ 1958 Thunderbird Hardtop
★★★★★ 1959 Thunderbird Convertible
★★★★ 1959 Thunderbird Hardtop
★★★★★ 1960 Thunderbird Convertible
★★★★★ 1960 Thunderbird Sunroof
★★★★ 1960 Thunderbird Hardtop

Not long after the first two-seater Thunderbirds started to hit the streets, Ford's designers, engineers, and product planners went back to their drawing boards to work on the little Thunderbird's successor.

Although the new Thunderbird was very popular and Ford sold every one it could build, most of the company's decision makers knew that the two-seat Thunderbird was limited in scope and sales potential. To increase its market share, the Thunderbird needed to grow from a smallish, sporty car into a car that could seat more than two people. The bottom line was that it needed room for a back seat. Thus was born the concept that would grow into a car nicknamed the "Squarebird." Over the course of the next two years, more than $30 million would be spent developing a larger, heavier, more luxurious Thunderbird.

1958

The new hardtop 1958 Thunderbird made its public debut on January 13, 1958, exactly one month after the last two-seat Thunderbird had rolled off the line. (Convertibles would not be built until June 1958, and because of that late showing, only 2,134 1958 convertibles were produced, compared to 35,758 hardtops.) The difference between the old and new Thunderbird was like night and day. The new car was some 18in longer and 1,000lb heavier than the Thunderbird it replaced.

The new 1958 Thunderbird was much larger and more square than the model it replaced. A sharp contrast, wouldn't you say? *Ford Motor Company*

The 1958 Thunderbirds were built at a just-opened assembly plant in Wixom, Michigan, alongside Lincoln's new Continentals. In addition to plant space, the two automobiles shared Ford's new unitized body construction. Unitized bodies were much stronger and less prone to flex and rattles than their body-on-frame predecessors.

The new Thunderbird was very square-looking compared to the first-generation cars, which probably explains the origin of its nickname. The exterior also looked more sculpted than it had on the original Thunderbird. In front, a set of dual headlights sat atop a massive bumper that housed the grille panel. Out back, a sculpted deck lid separated two taillight pods each housing two large taillights. On the car's sides, a power spear ran from the doors back to the taillights and helped give the car some depth and character.

The interiors of the new Thunderbirds were also now quite a bit different. The single

The 1958 Thunderbird showroom catalog featured a large Thunderbird crest on its cover. Was the 1958 Thunderbird really "America's Most Individual Car" of that year?

bench seat of the 1955–1957 cars was replaced by two front bucket seats separated by a full-length console and a rear bench seat whose upholstery emulated the look of the front

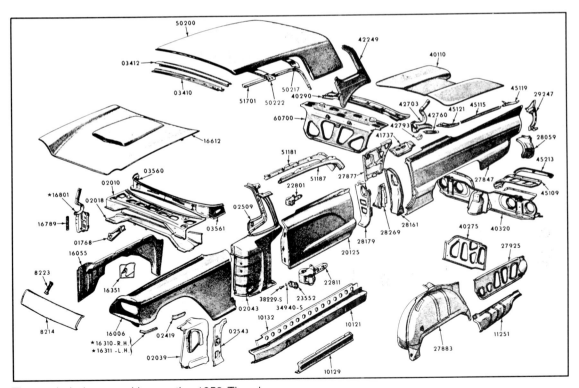

The myriad pieces making up the 1958 Thunderbird. *Ford Motor Company*

Here is a magazine ad for the 1958 Thunderbird convertible. The text mentions that an optional 375hp engine was available. There was a 375hp version of the Lincoln 430 engine that year. Could this mean that some 430 engines found their way into 1958 Thunderbirds?

Here's another 1958 Thunderbird magazine ad. This one mentions nothing about engine choices.

buckets. The console sat atop a high transmission/driveshaft tunnel that allowed the Thunderbird to sit as low as the earlier cars even

though it was quite a bit larger. Other changes made to the interior included a dual-pod dashboard layout, molded door and side panels, and some new trim pieces.

Under the hood, Ford pared down the Thunderbird's engine choices to just one. Ford deemed that the 300hp 352ci Thunderbird V-8 provided more than enough power

1958 Options	
Power brakes	$37
Overdrive transmission	$108
Power windows	$101
Four-way adjustable seat	$64
Tube-type radio	$77
Signal-seeking radio	$99
Whitewall tires (5)	$36
Tinted glass	$20
Windshield washers	$12
Backup lights	$10
Power steering	$69
Heater and defroster	$95
Leather interior	$106

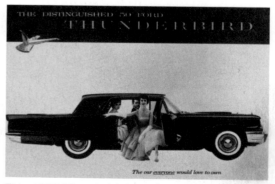

This 1959 Thunderbird catalog cover featured a distinctive-looking black hardtop on its cover.

A couple of nesting Thunderbirds in western Texas in 1992. For 1959, the front end wore horizontal grille bars instead of 1958's honeycomb design.

These two 1959 models look like they could fly again with a little TLC.

to move the Thunderbird. The base transmission was still a three-speed manual unit with a column-mounted shifter. An overdrive unit and a Fordomatic transmission were each available as extra-cost options. Despite the ex-

tra cost, most 1958 Thunderbird buyers opted for the Fordomatic.

The auto industry suffered a recession in 1958, making it a particularly tough year to introduce a new design. Despite this, the Ford

The late George Walker, Ford Motor Company design consultant, posing with a new 1959 Thunderbird with a 1919 Model T Ford in the background.

The forty-year difference in age and attitudes is readily apparent in this promotional photo. *Ford Motor Company*

A 1959 Thunderbird convertible in a top-down state. This particular photo shows its taillights and taillight grilles in detail. *Ford Motor Company*

Thunderbird actually posted a sales increase. All in all, the 1958 Thunderbirds were impressive cars, garnering many accolades from the automotive press, including the coveted *Motor Trend* "Car of the Year" award.

1959

Although the 1959 Thunderbirds had much in common with the 1958 models, there were enough changes to lure even more customers into the Thunderbird fold.

1959

Interior

Blue Sof textured vinyl bolster with blue nylon check fabric center
Green Sof textured vinyl bolster with green nylon check fabric center
Turquoise Sof textured vinyl bolster with turquoise check fabric center
Raven Sof textured vinyl bolster with Raven and white nylon check fabric center
Blue Sof textured vinyl bolster and Blue Sof textured vinyl center

Options

SelectShift Cruise-O-Matic transmission	$242
Overdrive transmission	$145
Power brakes	$43
Power steering	$75
Four-way power seat (Driver)	$86
Power windows	$102
Heavy-duty 70amp battery	$8
Fresh air heater and defroster	$83
Push-button AM radio	$105
SelectAire air conditioner	$446
Front seat belts	$23
Backup lights	$10
Tinted glass	$38
Windshield washers	$14
Outside rearview mirror	$5
Two-tone paint treatment	$26
Full wheel covers	$17
Fender skirts	$27
Five 814 rayon whitewall tires	$36
Thunderbird 430ci engine	$177
Leather interior	$106

The front honeycomb mesh grille of the 1958 Thunderbird was redesigned to a pattern of horizontal bars—an easy distinguishing point for the two model years. The side trim power spear was also changed. In 1958, a set of hash marks had trimmed the spear, but on the 1959 models the trim was changed to look like an arrowhead, and the Thunderbird script, formerly located on the front fender in front of the wheelwell, was moved down and placed on the side spear. Chassis and driveline changes on the 1959 model included replacing the coil-sprung rear end with one that was suspended on two longitudinal leaf springs and the addition of a more powerful engine. This 430ci extra-cost optional engine was rated at 350hp and could only be paired with Ford's new SelectShift Cruise-O-Matic transmission.

Thunderbird sales increased again in 1959, with a final production tally of 57,195 hardtops and 10,261 convertibles.

1960

For 1960, the Thunderbird still used the same body as the 1958 and 1959 cars. A new option, however, offered the best of both hardtop and convertible models. This option was a manually operated sunroof panel for the hardtop, which gave the open-air feeling of a convertible without the associated prob-

Ever wonder what is on the underside of a 1959–1960 Thunderbird convertible trunk lid? Here we see some relays, some wiring, and a solenoid or two, which control the up-and-down movement of this lid.

A load of new 1960 Lincolns and a lonely Ford Thunderbird on their way to a dealership. *Dick Copello Collection*

Ford offered a chrome engine dress-up kit for the 1960 Thunderbird. Here we see the chrome-plated air cleaner lid and valve covers that were part of the kit.

Judging by the 1958 Thunderbird and the clay mockup of the 1960 Ford in the background, it's likely that this styling exercise was done for the 1960 Thunderbird.

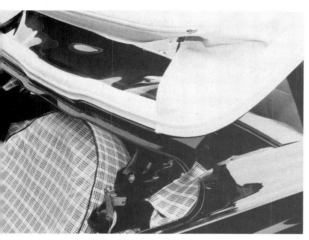

The spare tire, under a cover here, is in an awkward position in the trunks of 1958-1960 Thunderbirds.

A neat option on some 1960 Thunderbirds was a manually operated factory sunroof. Here you see the sunroof panel in the open position.

lems. This option was ordered in 2,536 Thunderbirds in 1960, and it is a highly sought-after item among collectors today.

Few changes were made to the Thunderbird in 1960, but some of these make it easy to distinguish a 1960 from the two previous model years. Ford changed the grille again, this time using a square hole mesh to provide a background to a horizontal and vertical bar

An admirer stops to look over a loaded 1960 Thunderbird convertible at a Massachusetts car show in 1992.

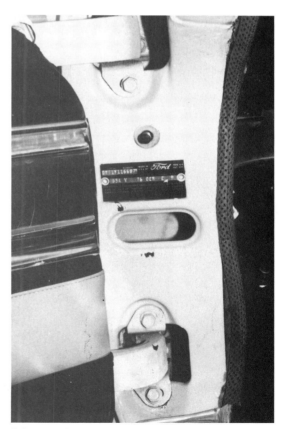

A factory data plate mounted on the left cowl pillar on a 1960 Thunderbird.

A new 1960 Thunderbird body joins some others going down the Wixom, Michigan, assembly line in 1960. *Ford Motor Company*

arrangement. The gunsight fender ornaments were changed to a design of clear Lucite plastic into which a Thunderbird emblem was positioned. A large Thunderbird emblem was also placed on the roof "C" panel, replacing the two small medallions used previously. Three hash marks were used to trim the rear

An inside shot of the handle which operates the factory sunroof in the 1960 Thunderbird. This panel is shown in the closed position.

1960
Exterior Colors and Codes

Corinthian White (A)	Platinum (F)
Gunpowder Gray (O)	Monte Carlo Red (I)
Raven Black (B)	Moroccan Ivory (P)
Briarcliff Green (N)	Springdale Rose (R)
Royal Burgundy (Q)	Palm Springs Rose (S)
Beachwood Brown (J)	Aquamarine (H)
Skymist Blue (C)	Sultana Turquoise (G)
Meadowvale Green (D)	Adriatic Green (E)
Kingston Blue (K)	Acapulco Blue (L)
Diamond Blue (M)	

Options

SelectShift Cruise-O-Matic transmission	$242
Overdrive transmission	$144.50
Master Guide power steering	$75.30
Swift Sure power brakes	$43.20
Power windows	$102.10
Power driver's seat	$92.10
Central console radio	$112.80
MagicAire heater	$82.90
SelectAire air conditioner	$465.80
Sliding sunroof	$212.40
Tinted glass	$37.90
Outside rearview mirror	$5.10
Rear fender skirts	$26.60
Aquamatic windshield washers	$13.70
Safety seat belts	$22.80
Backup lights	$9.50
Five whitewall tires	$35.70
Leather seat trim	$106.20
Heavy-duty battery	$7.60
Two-tone paint	$25.80
Thunderbird 430ci V-8 engine	$177

Door panel, trim, and seat details in a 1960 Thunderbird hardtop.

quarter panels, while the arrowhead trim pieces were deleted from the power bulge. Another change involved the taillight treatment; the 1960 models used three small taillights per side instead of two large taillights.

The changes made to the 1960 Thunderbird, though fairly minor, really freshened up the car's look and helped Ford sell even more of them. Company records show that for 1960, the Squarebird's final year, 80,398 hardtops and 11,860 convertibles were produced.

In 1958-1960 Thunderbirds equipped with factory air conditioning, the controls were located down on the console, while the vents were located above the radio in the middle of the dashboard.

A pre-production 1960 Thunderbird promotional photograph. Note that this car is wearing wheel covers from a 1960 Ford Galaxie. *Ford Motor Company*

A 1960 Thunderbird sunroof hardtop wearing Kelsey-Hayes wire wheels. *Ford Motor Company*

Danny Deaver owns this 1960 Thunderbird sunroof hardtop, shown here at the Albuquerque Country Club. This car is one of only 2,536 produced that year.

This 1960 Thunderbird sunroof hardtop ad shows a woman filming a military review. This is one page of a two-page ad that appeared in magazines in 1960. *Jerry Bougher Ads*

Chapter 4

1961-1963: Sporty Roadsters, and Projectile Thunderbirds

★★★★★ 1962 Thunderbird Sport Roadster

★★★★★ 1962 Thunderbird Sport Roadster "M" Engine

★★★★★ 1963 Thunderbird Sport Roadster

★★★★★ 1963 Thunderbird Sport Roadster "M" Engine

★★★★ 1963 Special Edition Landau

★★★★ 1961-1963 Thunderbird Convertible

★★★ 1962-1963 Thunderbird Landau

★★★ 1961-1963 Thunderbird Hardtop

In the late-1950s, Americans were becoming fascinated with rocketry, jet propulsion, and space travel. This interest really picked up when the Russians beat us into space with their Sputnik program of 1957. Some auto manufacturers took this "space" interest to heart and tried to incorporate aeronautics in their designs. Nowhere was this more evident than at the Ford Design Studios, where work was being done on a new Thunderbird design scheduled for release in the 1961 model year.

From its pointed front fenders to its jet pod rear end, this new "projectile" Thunderbird looked like a rocket. It was bold and brassy and a bit futuristic compared to the conservatively designed Squarebird it was replacing. The difference between the design of

The 1961 Thunderbirds featured a projectile design that was in marked contrast to the squared, formal look of the previous models.

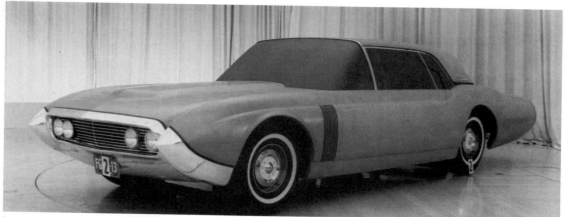

Now *this* is a massive front bumper and grille assembly.

Before this styling proposal was picked for the new 1961 Lincoln Continental, Ford planned to use it for the redesigned 1961 Thunderbird.

Believe it or not, this futuristic-looking clay model that looks like a rocket ship on wheels is said to be the first styling exercise for the 1961 Thunderbird.

the Squarebird and this new Thunderbird was just as drastic as the changeover from the 1957 to the 1958 models.

1961

The 1961 Thunderbirds were all new from stem to stern—new bodies, new bumpers, new trim, new taillights, and even a new engine. Ford bored and stroked its 352ci engine, to come up with a new 390ci engine. Although both engines put out 300hp, the 390 produced its power with much less stress. The optional 430ci Thunderbird engine of 1959 and 1960 was dropped, along with the manual transmissions. From 1961 until the 1980s, the SelectShift Cruise-O-Matic transmission would be the standard and only transmission offered on the Thunderbird.

The new Thunderbird was again offered in hardtop or convertible form. Base price was $4,170 for the hardtop and $4,637 for the convertible. Both of these prices were $400–$500 more than the prices of comparable 1960 models. The factory sunroof option was dropped, not to return until the late-1960s.

These new Thunderbirds made quite an impression on the public. New Thunderbirds were chosen frequently as contest prizes, and a gold 1961 Thunderbird convertible was selected as the pace car for the 50th Anniversary of the Indy 500 race.

A new option on these Thunderbirds was the Swing-Away steering column. This movable steering column allowed for easier entry and exit. At a mere $25, this option was quite a bargain considering the extra comfort and convenience it provided.

Production figures for the 1961 Thunderbird were down from those of 1960. Perhaps buyers didn't like the less conservative looks

One of the new features found on the 1961 Thunderbirds was a 390ci engine, as shown here. *Peter Sessler*

Judging by the wide whitewall tires and the projectile styling of its front fenders, this proposal was probably an early rendition of the 1961–63 Thunderbird.

of the new Thunderbird. When the last 1961 models rolled off the Wixom assembly line, 62,535 hardtops and 10,516 convertibles had been produced.

1962

Minimal changes were made for 1962. One of the changes involved the rear quarter panel trim. In 1961, this trim consisted of a series of thin, horizontal bars that were placed one above the other. For 1962, this trim was changed to a series of three ribbed hash marks placed one behind the other. Character lines had been punched into the hood on 1961 models, but were dropped from the 1962

models. The taillights between the two model years show some minor trim changes also.

Ford wanted to widen the Thunderbird's appeal and decided that what was needed was a more extensive lineup. In keeping with this strategy, two new models were added.

The first was a hardtop called the Landau, featuring a vinyl-covered top to distinguish it from the regular Thunderbird hardtop.

The second was called the Convertible Sports Roadster and was released as part of Ford's "Lively Ones" campaign. This model was meant to appeal to enthusiasts who longed for the return of the two-seater Thun-

Another 1961 Thunderbird/Continental styling exercise featured a grille treatment similar to that used on the 1963–65 Buick Riviera.

Some 1961 Thunderbirds were given away as prizes to racing champions, as this vintage Hurst Performance Products ad shows.

A serene setting was chosen for this advertisement, showing a couple cruising down a country lane in their new Thunderbird convertible. *Jerry Bougher Ads*

Here we have another look at one of the original styling exercises for the 1961 Thunderbird. Sometime just after this photo was taken the decision was made that this would be the 1961 Lincoln Continental.

This styling exercise for the 1961 Thunderbird shows some parking light "eyebrows" placed above the headlights. Did you notice that the hood on this car looks different than that chosen for the production car?

derbird. The Sports Roadster had a fiberglass tonneau cover that could be placed over the back seat to recreate the flavor of the original Thunderbird. With the top down and the tonneau cover in place, this new Thunderbird looked quite rakish. Its sporting look was further enhanced by such Sports Roadster-standard equipment as a set of chrome-plated Kelsey-Hayes wire wheels, a grab bar on the passenger side of the dashboard, and unique "Sports Roadster" insignias on the front fenders and between the streamlined headrests on the tonneau cover. The rear fender skirts were deleted when Kelsey-Hayes wire wheels were fitted because the wheels rubbed them. Not that it mattered, the open-wheel look of the rear fenders only further contributed to the Sports Roadster's sleek look.

The 300hp 390 was still the base Thunderbird engine, but starting in January 1962 and running through December 1962, Ford offered an optional V-8 engine for those Thunderbird drivers desiring a little extra power. Ford called this engine the 390 Sports V-8. In

With its fiberglass tonneau cover in place, the new-for-1962 Thunderbird Sports Roadster was a sleek, racy-looking automobile. This photograph was taken at Ford's Dearborn test track. *Ford Motor Company*

Here's an example of an early-1962 Ford show-room catalog.

Some of the unique features found on the Thunderbird Sports Roadster are these Kelsey-Hayes wire wheels and the unique Sports Roadster fender emblem.

the collector hobby, this engine is known as the "M" engine because that is the engine code it carries.

The M engine displaced 390ci, as did the regular "Z" code Thunderbird 390, but it differed from its tamer counterpart in carburetion and compression ratio. Instead of one Holley 4-barrel carburetor, the M engine used three Holley 2-barrel carburetors mounted backwards on a special cast-aluminum intake manifold. The Z engine's compression ratio was rated at 9.6:1, whereas the M engine's compression ratio was 10.6:1. Other equipment found on the M engine included a spe-cial cast-aluminum, low-restriction air cleaner and a chrome dress-up package that consisted of valve covers, oil dipstick handle, oil breather cap, radiator expansion tank, fuel log, master cylinder cap, and power steering reservoir cover. Ford rated the M engine at 340hp and charged a very reasonable $242.10 for it as an option. Still, only 300 cars between both model years came out of the factory with this engine.

Is this a styling proposal for a Thunderbird convertible or one for a "Landau" hardtop? The top looks like one that would be used on a convertible; however, all that chrome trim would be impractical.

1962

Prices

Hardtop	$4,321
Convertible	$4,788
Landau Convertible	$4,398
Sports Roadster	$5,439

Standard Equipment

300hp 390 4-barrel V-8
SelectShift Cruise-O-Matic transmission
Power brakes
Power steering
Padded instrument panel and visors
Electric windshield wipers
MagicAire heater and defroster
Electric clock
Console
Full wheel covers
Undercoating
Backup lights
Parking brake warning lamp
Glove box and ashtray lights
Courtesy lights
Luggage compartment light
Movable steering column

Exterior Colors

Raven Black	Acapulco Blue
Caspian Blue	Cascade Green

Tucson Yellow
Heritage Burgundy
Rangoon Red
Fieldstone Tan
Chalfonte Blue
Deep Sand Blue

Skymist Blue
Chestnut
Sandshell Beige
Sahara Rose
Patrician Green

Convertible Top Colors: Black, Blue, White

Options

"M" engine 390ci 3x2-barrel	$242.10
SelectAire air conditioner	$415.10
Heavy-duty 70amp battery	$7.60
Fender skirts	$26.60
Tinted glass	$43
Two-tone paint	$25.80
Automatic speed control	$80.50
Power windows	$106.20
Deluxe wheel covers with simulated knock-off hubs	$15.60
Kelsey-Hayes wire wheels	$373.30
Windshield washers	$13.70
Five whitewall 8x14in four-ply rayon tires	$42.10
Five whitewall 8x14in four-ply nylon tires	$70.40
Automatic vacuum door locks	$34.10
Leather seat trim	$106.20
Power driver's seat	$92.10
Power passenger seat	$92.10
AM radio	$83.10
Front seat belts	$16.80
Rear seat reverberating speaker	$15.50

1963

For 1963, the Thunderbird's body was revamped with the addition of a windsplit character line that ran from just behind the headlights on the front fenders to the rear of the doors where the line turned downward. Just below this character line on the doors was a series of hash mark trim pieces. This restyling

The 1963 Thunderbird Sports Roadster, like its 1962 counterpart, was a sleek-looking automobile when its top was down and its fiberglass tonneau cover was in place. *Ford Motor Company*

There is only One Thunderbird !

... Which one is the Grand Prix?

Catalina   Starfire

Grand Prix   Chevrolet

One of the Thunderbird's chief competitors in 1963 was the Pontiac Grand Prix. This special brochure was prepared for Ford salesmen to show how their product compared to the competition.

There wasn't too much spare room in the trunk of a 1961-1963 Thunderbird convertible, as this photo clearly shows. *Peter Sessler*

makes it easy to tell the 1963 models from similar 1961 and 1962 Thunderbirds.

Once again, Ford offered four distinct models in the Thunderbird line: hardtop, convertible, Landau, and Sports Roadster. Base prices started at $4,542 for the hardtop and peaked at $5,660 for the Sports Roadster.

Ford also offered a limited-edition Landau model introduced to the public in Monaco in January 1963 (hence, its "Monaco Landau" tag in the hobby). These Thunderbirds were finished off in a white exterior color with a special rose-beige-colored vinyl roof. Special Landau "S" bars were mounted on the roof's side panels. Their interiors featured white leather seat coverings, rose-beige carpeting, simulated rosewood trim appliqués, and white steering wheels and steering columns. Simulated knock-off spinner wheel covers completed the special look. Over the

Here's a vinyl top treatment that hasn't been tried on a production model. The designers involved with this 1963 proposal used an elongated Thunderbird

"Landau" roof bar to separate the vinyl covering from the non-covered area.

1963 Prices

Hardtop	$4,542	Landau edition (limited)	$200
Landau hardtop	$4,645	Two-tone paint	$25.80
Convertible	$5,009	Four-way power driver's seat	$92.10
Sports Roadster	$5,660	Four-way passenger seat	$92.10
		Power windows	$106.20
Options		AM/FM radio	$83.70
SelectAire air conditioner	$415.10	Front seat belts	$16.80
Heavy-duty 70amp battery	$7.60	Rear seat speakers (hardtops)	$15.50
Automatic (vacuum) door locks	$34.10	Deluxe wheel covers	$15.60
Fender skirts	$26.60	Windshield washers	$13.70
Tinted glass	$43	Chrome wire wheels (standard on	
Leather seat trim	$106.20	Sports Roadster)	$373.30
		Five 8x14in four-ply rated rayon whitewall tires	$42.10
		Five 8x14in four-ply rated nylon whitewall tires	$70.40

course of the next six months or so, Ford built 2,000 of these limited-production cars. Each featured a "Special Edition Landau" plaque—numbered between 1 and 2,000—on its console panel just below the heater controls.

Even though the 1963 Thunderbird line offered more variety and more equipment than in previous model years, production and sales were down in this the last year of the Projectile Thunderbirds.

This Thunderbird showcar, dubbed *Constellation*, featured a fastback roof with a rear window similar to that used on early Plymouth Barracudas. The roof also looks like it has been fitted with gullwing panels.

The Budd Connection

From 1954 through 1960, the Automotive Division of the Budd Corporation provided 250,000 Thunderbird bodies to Ford. Ford began stamping out its own bodies for the 1961 model year, and the loss of such a contract must have had quite an effect on Budd.

Although the larger Thunderbirds were more successful from a sales standpoint than the original two-seat model, there were still some people at Ford Motor Company who, in the early-1960s, wanted to resurrect the two-seater Thunderbird concept. These people weren't satisfied with the Sports Roadster models that offered the sportiness and flavor of the smaller Thunderbirds. For them, no pretender would do; it had to be the real McCoy.

These people made their feelings known to upper management. The idea showed some merit, so a study group was initiated to investigate the feasibility of bringing back the two-seater Thunderbird. In 1962, a group was formed between Ford and Budd employees to work on this project. Budd was very interested in this idea because it still had the original 1957 Thunderbird body stamping dies and thought, with some slight modifications, that the 1957 Thunderbird bodies could be updated and provided to Ford at a reasonable cost. These updates included rounding the tops of the front fenders, removing the rear fins, extending the wheelbase, and mounting the modified body on top of a Falcon platform. On the inside, a single, small jump seat was to be added to carry small children, making this Thunderbird a family car of sorts.

Budd produced a working prototype called the "XT-Bird," which was well received. When push came to shove, however, the idea was rejected by Iacocca. What was his rationale for turning down this concept when it seemed to have so much going for it? Nobody can say for sure, but it might have had something to do with the Mustang program which was pretty well advanced by that time. Though the XT-Bird never made it past the prototype stage, it did share something in common with the Mustang: both sporty looking automobiles were draped over Falcon platforms.

This two-page 1963 Thunderbird magazine ad shows the complete 1963 Thunderbird lineup, including the Thunderbird convertible, Sports Roadster, Landau, and a Thunderbird hardtop in the background. *Jerry Bougher Ads*

Only 2,000 1963 Limited-Edition Landau Thunderbird hardtops were made available for purchase, as this ad clearly shows. The car in the ad is posed in front of the Monaco landmark where these cars were officially introduced. *Jerry Bougher Ads*

"How to Catch a Thunderbird" is a clever way to promote the Thunderbird Sports Roadster for 1963. This ad showed a red car set against a grassy, green background. *Jerry Bougher Ads*

The Thunderbird *Italien* showcar, with its racy fast-back roof design, was a popular attraction in Ford's

Custom Caravan and appeared at car shows from coast-to-coast during 1963 and 1964.

One of the features found on the Thunderbird
Sports Roadster was a chrome-plated engine
dress-up kit, as shown here.

This photograph shows a design proposal for a
half-vinyl "Landau" roof treatment.

You can never tell where a nice-looking Thunderbird convertible will turn up. This 1963 model participated in a car show in Sydney, Australia. Sydney even has a Thunderbird club to help promote the Thunderbird Spirit "down under."

In 1963, Ford used many clever ads to promote the Thunderbird, such as this "What to Tell Your Wife Before the Thunderbird Comes." *Jerry Bougher Ads*

Not all Thunderbirds have led a pampered life. Judging from the "14" on the door, this 1962 hardtop, found in an abandoned junkyard in New Mexico, spent some time as a racer.

PATENT PLATE INFORMATION FOR MODEL AND EQUIPMENT

EXPLANATION OF CODES

63A	Body Type (2-Door Hardtop)
J	Exterior Paint Color
85	Type and Color of Interior Trim
27H	Assembly Date (27th Day of August)
101 11	Dealer Special Order
1	Rear Axle Ratio (3.00 to 1)
4	Transmission Type (Cruise-O-Matic)

VEHICLE WARRANTY NUMBER   3 Y 83 Z 100001

3 — Last Digit of Model Year (1963). Y — Assembly Plant (Wixom). 83 — Patent Plate Code for 2-Door Hardtop Model. Z — Engine Model (390 V-8, 4-V). 100001 — Each assembly plant numbers cars in consecutive order, beginning with 100001 each model year.

COLOR CODE

Refer to Interior-Exterior Trim Combination Chart for code numbers. If a special paint is used, the color space on the patent plate will not be stamped.

TRIM CODE

Refer to Interior-Exterior Trim Combination Chart for code numbers. Deviation trim sets use existing trim codes plus a suffix. A numerical suffix denotes trim that is not serviced, and an alphabetical suffix denotes trim that is serviced.

DATE CODE

A	January	D	April	G	July	K	October
B	February	E	May	H	August	L	November
C	March	F	June	J	September	M	December

DSO CODE

Domestic special orders, foreign special orders, and preapproved special orders have the complete order number stamped on the plate. If the unit is regular production, the DSO space on the plate will not be stamped.

AXLE CODE

The conventional rear axle ratio is denoted by numerical code.

1 — 3.00 to 1 Axle Ratio

TRANSMISSION CODE

The numeral "4" is the code for Cruise-O-Matic — Thunderbird's standard transmission.

ENGINE CODE

Engines for domestic service are denoted by the use of code letters. Numerals are used for export engines only.

M — 390-Cubic-Inch, V-8, 6-V   Z — 390-Cubic-Inch, V-8, 4-V   9 — 390-Cubic-Inch, V-8, 4-V

ASSEMBLY PLANT CODE

The letter "Y" is the designation for the Thunderbird Assembly Plant in Wixom, Michigan.

The patent plate worn by every Thunderbird provides a wealth of information including where the car was built, when, engine size, and color and trim codes. A 1963 plate and how to decipher it is shown. *Ford Motor Company*

Chapter 5

1964-1966: Back to the Square Look

★★★★★ 1966 Thunderbird Convertible
★★★★★ 1965 Thunderbird Convertible
★★★★★ 1964 Thunderbird Convertible
★★★★ 1965 Thunderbird Special Landau
★★★★ 1964 Thunderbird Landau
★★★★ 1966 Thunderbird Town Landau
★★★★ 1965 Thunderbird Landau
★★★ 1966 Thunderbird Town Hardtop
★★★ 1966 Thunderbird Hardtop
★★★ 1964 Thunderbird Hardtop
★★★ 1965 Thunderbird Hardtop

The styling pendulum swung back to the conservative side for the fourth series of Thunderbirds introduced in the fall of 1963 as 1964 models. They looked a lot like the 1958–1960 Squarebirds and completely different from Projectile Thunderbirds that preceded them. Gone was the rocket ship look, replaced by a squared-off conservative look that would appeal to a much wider audience—at least according to corporate wisdom. A new bumper and grille arrangement, new fenders, headlights, hood, and hoodscoop adorned the front. On the sides, new upper- and lower-body character lines—more muted but still reminiscent of the fins of the 1950s—helped give the car a sculpted look. Ford even reworked the top and glass areas to look differ-

ent from those found on the 1961–1963 cars. At the back, there was a new bumper and a set of rectangular taillights, as well as a restyled trunk lid that covered a larger trunk area than was offered on previous models.

The venerable 390ci Thunderbird V-8 was the only powerplant offered for Thunderbirds in 1964. It still carried a horsepower rating of 300 and a torque rating of 427lb-ft, more than enough power and torque to move 4,500lb of Thunderbird bulk down the road smartly.

This styling department photograph from 1961 shows a design for the 1964 Thunderbird. The front clip looks similar to what actually appeared on the production model; however, the rear quarter panel looks like that used on the Continentals of the period.

People who Thunderbird move in a special atmosphere

This 1964 Thunderbird ad with a hardtop model shown set in a serene background gives the impression that Thunderbird people are a special group. *Jerry Bougher Ads*

1964 THUNDERBIRD . . . offers far more than

1964 Buick Riviera . . . or

1964 Pontiac Grand Prix

This review brochure was prepared for Ford salesmen so they could compare the Thunderbird favorably against its Buick Riviera and Pontiac Grand Prix competition.

A Ford promotional photograph of a new 1964 Thunderbird convertible. Looking inside, we can see the top of the rear coved seat, which would become a Thunderbird trademark. *Ford Motor Company*

Here's a ragtag conglomeration of parts. This 1961 Thunderbird features unique front fender trim, a gullwing-type top, and a 1964–66 Thunderbird door.

Once again, the SelectShift Cruise-O-Matic transmission was the only transmission offered.

Although the engineers had changed little in the driveline, it was a different story inside the car. Most noticeable of the interior changes involved the seating. A pair of thin-shell bucket seats replaced the former large, bulky seats in the front, and there was a new, optional reclining passenger bucket seat with a fold-down back.

The rear bench seat was also redesigned. Rather than having a distinct edge where the seat's side and door panel met, this seat back curved around much like some couches. Ford called this design a "coved rear seat"; the motivation behind its design was that the passengers could sit sideways to gain more leg

This magazine ad shows an open convertible model with a hardtop in the background. Note the dashboard details and the Swing-Away steering wheel. *Jerry Bougher Ads*

A Thunderbird wheel cover with a spinner, as found on some 1964 and 1965 Thunderbirds. Also note the thin whitewall band on the tire. *Peter Sessler*

Here we see an "S" Landau bar, as used on the 1964-1965 Thunderbird Landaus. In the photo, you can also see the rear coved seat found in this era of Thunderbirds. *Peter Sessler*

This close-up shot of a Kelsey-Hayes wire wheel shows why these beautiful wheels are popular with Thunderbird enthusiasts. You'll find them on everything from a 1955 to 1960-era models. *Peter Sessler*

room. Whether this seat allowed that extra room is open to debate , but it was a nice gimmick that made the Thunderbird stand out from the competition. And for a car like the Thunderbird, anything special meant more sales.

Ford also redesigned the floor console and the dashboard. The most notable feature of the new dashboard was instrumentation that looked like it was taken right out of an airplane.

A new interior feature found in the 1964 Thunderbird hardtops was "Silent Flo" ventilation. This system drew fresh air through the

This shot of an open Thunderbird convertible trunk lid shows the hydraulic rams, switches, relays, and solenoids that make this power system work. *Peter Sessler*

Spare tire storage in a 1964-1966 Thunderbird convertible is still a bit cramped, but at least the tire is easier to get out than on earlier models. *Peter Sessler*

In the 1960s, AMT released some great Thunderbird model kits. This unbuilt kit is highly sought after by collectors today. *George Hinds Collection*

passenger compartment and vented it through a port system at the base of the rear window. Air drawn over the top and down the back window would pull this air out of the vents.

Only three Thunderbird models were offered in 1964: the hardtop, convertible, and Landau. The Sports Roadster had been dropped, but for the person who still wanted such a car, Ford offered a redesigned tonneau cover as a dealer- or customer-installed option. The price of this fiberglass cover was around $269. There were no special Sports Roadster insignias or a passenger assist bar for the interior this year. However, the chrome-plated Kelsey Hayes wire wheels that were part of the Sports Roadster package were still available for all Thunderbirds. These beautiful wheels offered a distinctive sporty look; 15in versions cost $373.10 for a

This beautiful 1965 Thunderbird convertible has been treated to a set of Kelsey-Hayes wire wheels and a factory tonneau cover. Both items give this car a racy look. *Peter Sessler*

set of four. (These wheels are very popular with Thunderbird enthusiasts and you see them on other model years, too.)

The restyled 1964 Thunderbirds found a receptive audience, and by the model year's end, 92,465 1964 Thunderbirds had been sold.

1964 Standard Equipment

300hp 390ci Thunderbird V-8
SelectShift Cruise-O-Matic transmission
Automatic parking brake release
Power steering
Swing-away steering column
Day/night inside mirror
Remote control exterior driver's mirror
Individually adjustable front bucket seats
Retractable front seat belts and reminder light
Rear center seat folding armrest
Padded instrument panel pad and sun visors
Transistorized AM radio
MagicAire heater and defroster
Electric clock
Courtesy lights
Backup lights
Trunk light
Variable-speed wipers
Windshield washers
Undercoating

Options

Sports tonneau cover
Automatic speed control
Kelsey-Hayes wire wheels
Sports tachometer
Power windows
White sidewall tires
Power seats
Full wheel covers with simulated knock-off hubs
SelectAire air conditioner
AM/FM radio
Tinted glass
Rear seat speakers
Fender skirts
Spotlight
Leather upholstery

Exterior Colors and Codes

(A) Raven Black
(B) Midnight Turquoise
(C) Honey Gold
(E) Silver Mink
(F) Arcadian Blue
(G) Pastel Yellow
(H) Caspian Blue
(J) Rangoon Red
(M) Wimbledon White
(N) Diamond Blue
(P) Prairie Bronze
(Q) Brittany Blue
(R) Ivy Green
(S) Charcoal Gray

(T) Navajo Beige
(U) Patrician Green
(W) Rose Beige
(X) Vintage Burgundy
(Z) Chantilly Beige
(4) Frost Turquoise

Convertible Top Colors and Codes

(A) Black
(B) White
(C) Tan
(D) Blue

Landau Vinyl Top Colors and Codes

(1) Black
(2) White
(3) Brown
(4) Blue

Interior Trim Options and Codes

Note: "Appointments" are carpets, dashpad coverings, and other interior trim pieces.
(12) Blue vinyl and cloth
(16) Black vinyl and cloth
(19) Palomino vinyl and cloth
(21) Silver Blue vinyl
(22) Blue vinyl
(23) Burgundy vinyl
(24) Beige vinyl
(25) Red vinyl
(26) Black vinyl
(27) Aqua vinyl
(28) Ivy Gold vinyl
(29) Palomino vinyl
(32) Blue leather option
(35) Red leather option
(36) Black leather option
(39) Palomino leather option
(G2) White vinyl with blue appointments
(G3) White vinyl with burgundy appointments
(G4) White vinyl with beige appointments
(G5) White vinyl with red appointments
(G6) White vinyl with black appointments
(G7) White vinyl with turquoise appointments
(G8) White vinyl with Ivy Gold appointments
(G9) White vinyl with Palomino appointments
(H2) White leather with blue appointments
(H3) White leather with burgundy appointments
(H4) White leather with beige appointments
(H5) White leather with red appointments
(H6) White leather with black appointments
(H7) White leather with turquoise appointments
(H8) White leather with Ivy Gold appointments
(H9) White leather with Palomino appointments

This was the second best year for Thunderbird sales to date, with only the 1960 models selling better. Sales wouldn't top this mark until well into the 1970s.

1965

The most notable changes Ford made to the 1965 Thunderbird line involved the addition of new safety equipment, including power-assisted Kelsey-Hayes disc brakes at the front end. Earlier Thunderbirds had not been known for their braking prowess, but the discs changed that. Added bonuses included less brake fade, because disc brakes run cooler than drum units, and safer stopping in wet conditions. Disc brake-equipped 1965 Thunderbirds could outperform any drum-braked Thunderbird in any braking situation.

Another safety-related item was the taillights, which now featured a sequential turn signal feature. The taillight housing was divided into segments, each of which was fitted with a bulb. When the turn signal lever was moved, the corresponding taillight would light up starting at the inside and moving to the outside. This novel idea grabbed the attention of following drivers better than a standard turn signal, thus decreasing the risk of a rear end collision.

Although minor, other changes also deserve mention. On the front grille, vertical trim bars were added to the horizontal bar motif used before. The name "Thunderbird" was removed from both the leading edge of the hood and the trim plate separating the two taillights, and was replaced with stylized Thunderbird emblems. Ford also removed the Thunderbird emblems from the taillight lenses. Now the taillight lenses featured a series of vertical trim to help highlight their sequential blinking feature.

Another change to the 1965 Thunderbird was the piece of trim added to the front fenders. This trim was styled to simulate a vent and is the easiest feature to spot that differentiates between the 1964 and 1965 Thunder-

This shot of a 1965 Thunderbird engine compartment shows its 390ci engine, factory air conditioner compressor, disc brake master cylinder, and a radiator expansion tank. *Peter Sessler*

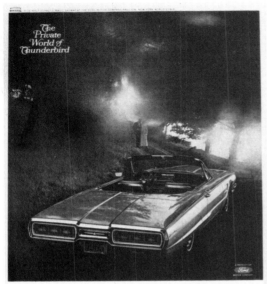

This "Private World of Thunderbird" ad shows a new 1965 convertible in an ethereal setting. *Jerry Bougher Ads*

Here is an example of a regional ad used by the New England Ford Dealers Association. The ad shows the Limited Edition Landau model for 1965. *Paul McLaughlin Sr. Collection*

This front end shows a split grille arrangement and hide-away headlights. Judging by this photograph's date of 8-12-63, this was probably a proposal for the 1966 Thunderbird.

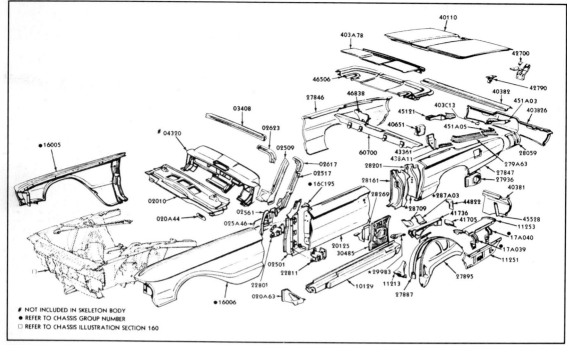

More than forty pieces made up the 1965 Thunderbird convertible. *Ford Motor Company*

birds. Other new features for 1965 included keyless door locking, reversible keys, a dome light for convertible models, door-mounted courtesy lights, and a new Thunderbird ornament on the roof's C panel.

Once again, the 1965 Thunderbird lineup consisted of three models: hardtop, convertible, and Landau. In addition, as in 1963, Ford offered in mid-year a limited-edition "Thunderbird Special Landau," featuring Emberglo

Although you probably can't see them in this photo, this 1966 Thunderbird prototype is wearing a set of clear, plexiglass headlight covers. Besides the headlight covers, its parking lights, grille treatment, grille ornament, and the name Thunderbird spelled out on the front of the hood weren't seen on the 1966 production cars.

1965 Prices

Hardtop	$4,584
Hardtop-Landau	$4,687
Convertible	$5,051

Options

Retracting power antenna	$29.60
Driver's four-way power seat	$92.10
Driver and passenger four-way power seat	$184.10
Power windows	$106.20
Power vent windows (includes charge for power windows)	$159.40
Safety convenience control panel	$58
Speed control system	$63.40
SelectAire air conditioner	$424.90
Heavy-duty battery (standard with air conditioner or transistorized ignition)	$7.60
Closed emission system (California-type)	$5.30
Remote deck lid release (hardtops only)	$12.90
Fender skirts	$32.70
Tinted glass with banded windshield	$43
Leather seat trim	$106.20
Limited slip differential	$47.70
Two-tone paint	$25.80
AM/FM radio and antenna	$83.70
Reclining passenger seat	$45.10
Rear seat radio speaker	$16.90
Rear seat studiosonic speaker	$54.10
Five whitewall 8.15x15in four-ply rated rayon tires with red band	$43.90
Transistorized ignition system	$76
Deluxe wheel covers	$15.60
Extra cooling package	$7.90
Heavy-duty suspension	$26.60

"The Private World of Thunderbird" was the theme that Ford used to help promote the 1965 Thunderbird. *Jerry Bougher Ads*

exterior paint, Parchment-colored vinyl roof covering, color-coordinated interior with woodgrain appliqués on the door and dashboard panels, and special color-coordinated wheel covers.

Despite all these refinements, sales were down from the previous year by 16,000 units.

1966

For 1966, several changes were made to the Thunderbird to make it more appealing. For openers Ford added two new models to the lineup and dropped one from the previous year. The two new models were the Town Landau and the Town Hardtop. The model dropped was the Landau.

These two new models featured a roof C-panel design that was wider than the regular hardtop. The latter featured rear quarter windows, while the stretched roof panel of the former covered up the area where these windows were located. The "Town" models offered a roof that was distinctive and enhanced the privacy of the rear seat occupants. The only drawback was that this roof created a large blind spot, especially on the car's right-hand side. The difference between the Town Hardtop and the Town Landau was that the Landau used a vinyl top covering and fancier interior appointments. Besides offering a couple of new models, Ford also offered the 1966 Thunderbird buyer a pretty nifty restyling job. Most of the redesign was carried out at the front end, where the hood, front fenders, bumper, and grille were either modified or changed outright. The Thunderbird's hood was lengthened, and the hoodscoop and its trim flattened out and updated. The longer hood caused the grille to jut out aggressively, an impression heightened by the large, cast Thunderbird emblem placed in its center. The bumper was redesigned and now included a splash pan underneath.

The idea behind these plexiglass headrests was to decrease wind buffeting of rear passengers.

This rear shot of a 1966 Thunderbird hardtop allows us to compare its top with the top used on the Town models. This top used a thinner roof "C" panel than the others.

A different-looking proposal for the 1966 Thunderbird Landau hardtop. Note the roof panel treatment and front fender trim.

Ford removed the simulated fender vent trim of the 1965 model, and the two-taillight arrangement used on the 1964 and 1965 models was replaced by a long, single unit that stretched from one side of the car to the other. Ford also changed the interior trim and the wheel covers.

The standard powerplant for the 1966 Thunderbird was still the venerable 390 Thunderbird V-8, now rated at 315hp. How-

ever, if that wasn't enough thunder for your 'Bird, Ford also offered a 428ci Thunderbird V-8 that was rated at 345hp.

This would be the last year for the Thunderbird convertible. Low sales of only 6,000–10,000 cars per year, impending government regulations about rollover protection, and other safety concerns made it difficult for Ford to rationalize keeping the "drop top" in the Thunderbird lineup.

The stylist that penned this 1966 Thunderbird in 1964 thought the car should have rectangular headlights. Though a popular accessory on show cars and prototypes during the 1960s, state laws kept rectangular headlights off cars sold to the public.

Scott Logan of Richfield, Minnesota, owns this beautiful 1966 Thunderbird Town hardtop. This car is loaded with just about every option the Thunderbird had that year. *Scott Logan*

Here is a Ford promotional photo of the 1966 Thunderbird Town Landau. These models featured wide roof "C" panels and a vinyl roof covering. *Ford Motor Company*

The Thunderbird Town models, Town hardtop and Town Landau, featured roofs with wider "C" panels than those used on the regular hardtop. *Scott Logan*

1966 Prices

Hardtop	$4,395.42
Convertible	$4,844.75
Town Hardtop	$4,451.89
Town Landau	$4,551.89

Options

428 4-barrel 345hp Thunderbird V-8
Six-way power driver's seat only
Six-way power driver and passenger seats
Power windows
Retracting power antenna
Heavy-duty battery
Limited slip differential
Transistorized ignition system
Highway pilot control
Safety convenience control panel
Tinted glass
SelectAire air conditioner
AM/FM radio
Remote deck lid release
Rear seat speaker
Reclining passenger seat
AM radio and StereoSonic eight-track tape system
Rear fender skirts
License plate frames
Leather seat trim
Two-tone paint
Whitewall tires
Wheel covers with simulated knock-off hubs

Colors and Codes

(A) Arcadian Blue
(H) Sahara Beige
(K) Nightmist Blue
(M) Wimbledon White
(P) Antique Bronze
(R) Ivy Green
(T) Candyapple Red
(U) Tahoe Turquoise
(V) Emberglo
(X) Vintage Burgundy
(Z) Sauterne Gold
(E) Silver Mink
(N) Diamond Blue
(G) Sapphire Blue
(Q) Brittany Blue
(O) Silver Rose
(B) Sunset Beige
(L) Honeydew Yellow
(2) Mariner Turquoise

Interior Options and Codes

Note: Appointments are carpets, console coverings, dashpad, and other interior trim pieces.

Code	Description
(21)	Silver Mink vinyl
(22)	Dark blue vinyl
(23)	Burgundy vinyl
(24)	Emberglo vinyl
(25)	Red vinyl
(26)	Black vinyl
(27)	Aqua vinyl
(28)	Ivy Gold vinyl
	White vinyl
	Parchment vinyl
(G1)	White vinyl with Silver Mink appointments
(G2)	White vinyl with blue appointments
(G3)	White vinyl with burgundy appointments
(G4)	White vinyl with Emberglo appointments
(G6)	White vinyl with black and white appointments
(G7)	White vinyl with turquoise appointments
(G8)	White vinyl with Ivy Gold appointments
(G9)	White vinyl with Palomino appointments
(B2)	Parchment vinyl with blue appointments
(B3)	Parchment vinyl with burgundy appointments
(B4)	Parchment vinyl with Emberglo appointments
(B6)	Parchment vinyl with black appointments
(B7)	Parchment vinyl with turquoise appointments
(B8)	Parchment vinyl with Ivy Gold appointments
(B9)	Parchment vinyl with Palomino appointments
(12)	Dark blue fabric
(16)	Black fabric
1D	Parchment fabric
62	Dark blue leather
65	Red leather
66	Black leather
L2	Parchment leather with blue appointments
L3	Parchment leather with burgundy appointments
L4	Parchment leather with Emberglo appointments
L6	Parchment leather with black appointments
L7	Parchment leather with turquoise appointments
L8	Parchment leather with Ivy Gold appointments
L9	Parchment leather with Palomino appointments

Ford didn't offer a Sports Roadster option in 1964 but they did offer a redesigned tonneau cover as an option for those who wanted one. *Ford Motor Company*

Now here is a different way to promote a car. You picture the car with some of its options in the sky above as a background. *Jerry Bougher Ads*

This promotional postcard shows an airline pilot in control of a 1966 Thunderbird Town Landau model. *George Hinds Collection*

Chapter 6

1967-1969: More Luxury and Some Additional Doors

Rating	Model
★★★★	1967 Thunderbird Two-door hardtop
★★★★	1967 Thunderbird Landau hardtop
★★★	1967 Thunderbird Landau four-door sedan
★★★★	1968 Thunderbird Two-door hardtop
★★★★	1968 Thunderbird Landau hardtop
★★★	1968 Thunderbird Landau four-door sedan
★★★★★	1969 Thunderbird Landau hardtop with sunroof
★★★★★	1969 Thunderbird Landau four-door sedan with sunroof
★★★★	1969 Thunderbird Landau hardtop
★★★★	1969 Thunderbird Two-door hardtop
★★★	1969 Thunderbird Landau four-door sedan

One of the perks of working at a Ford dealership as I did in the 1960s was the chance to see new cars before they were shown to the public. I remember back in September 1966 when we received our first 1967 Thunderbirds. This first load consisted of three two-door hardtops, one two-door Landau, and one four-door Landau. The two-door cars were all relegated to our back lot, but the four-door was driven right into the shop, where it was prepped, washed, and waxed and put on display. This car was Vintage Burgundy in color with a black vinyl top. If my memory is correct, it was equipped with a black leather interior. It was the plushest-looking Thunderbird I had ever seen, and it caused quite a stir among customers and staff alike. Whenever a customer would come into

our showroom during that time and ask to see a Thunderbird, he would be taken into the shop to see our "Burgundy Beauty," and then he would be taken out back to see the two-door models. I don't remember whether we sold many four-door Landau Thunderbirds

This Thunderbird styling proposal for the 1967 models looks like some Chrysler products of the late-1960s. The grille also looks like that used on the 1967–68 Mercury Cougars.

The 1967 Thunderbird lineup is presented in this factory promotional photograph. In the foreground is the new four-door Landau. *Ford Motor Company*

As you can see in this photograph dated 6-11-65, the 1967 Thunderbird two-door hardtop's styling was pretty much finalized a good fifteen months prior to production.

This styling exercise was an early proposal for the 1967 Thunderbird.

that year, but I can tell you that one particular four-door Landau still sticks out in my mind more than twenty-six years later.

Although the introduction of a four-door model, the first one for the line, certainly was the top news for the 1967 model year, other noteworthy changes occurred as well.

First of all, the new 1967 Thunderbirds were restyled from the front to rear, top to bottom, and inside out. Nothing on the interior or exterior was carried over from 1966. In fact, only in the drivetrain are there similarities between the two model years.

A wide-mouth grille cavity housing a mesh grille of horizontal and vertical pieces graced the front of the car. At the grille's ends were vacuum-operated doors each concealing twin headlamps. A large, redesigned Thunderbird emblem prominently occupied the center of the grille. Forming the lower portion of the grille cavity, a large, sculptured bumper wrapped around to protect the leading edges of the front fenders. Just behind the bumper on the lower-body edge, a piece of bright trim ran from the bumper to the leading edge of the front wheelwell; another piece of this trim ran between the front and rear wheelwells, and still another piece ran from the rear wheelwell to the rear bumper. These trim pieces helped tie together the front and rear ends.

Another feature of the 1967 Thunderbird was a long, thrusting hood combined with a

Did you know we make a 4-door Thunderbird? We didn't want anything to stand in your way.

Thunderbird
Unique in all the world

This is one of the magazine ads that Ford used to promote the 1967 Thunderbird four-door Landau. *Jerry Bougher Ads*

short rear deck, a design made popular by the Mustang. A redesigned top was another new feature and employed "unipane" or ventless side windows. The taillight was redesigned to

Another 1967 Thunderbird styling exercise looks quite a bit different than the production version which made its debut in fall 1966.

A "porthole"-type vinyl top is one of the unique features seen on this 1968 Thunderbird proposal.

Another 1967 Thunderbird prototype.

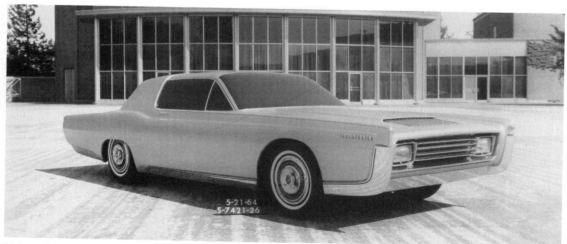

This styling proposal for the 1967 Thunderbird features a squared-off look like the mid-1960s Continental.

Here is a 1967 Thunderbird promotional postcard featuring the two-door hardtop. *Ford Motor Company*

A pair of models show how they feel about the new Thunderbird Landau four-door in this 1967 promotional postcard. *Ford Motor Company*

include sequential turn signals above a redesigned rear bumper.

The 1967 Thunderbird design featured large, full-radius wheelwells with no provisions for fender skirts (a first in Thunderbird history). A sculptured body character line ran from the rear end forward to the front wheelwell. To add a sporty look, Ford offered a new wheel cover with a radial spoke design.

Ford made several changes to the interiors of these cars, too, including redesigned front and rear seats, console, door panels, instruments, and instrument panel.

Ford returned to the body-on-frame construction Thunderbirds had used before the Squarebird came on line. This enabled Ford to cut the car's weight.

Ford was still very much interested in safety, and it equipped the Thunderbird with a redesigned, padded, impact-absorbing steering wheel center pad, and a new, dual reservoir master braking cylinder that amounted to a backup braking system.

The standard powerplant for the Thunderbird in 1967 was still the 315hp 4-barrel 390 V-8, with a 345hp 428 available as an extra-cost option. Behind both engines was Ford's excellent C6 SelectShift Cruise-O-Matic transmission.

Another 1967 Thunderbird prototype. This one features a rear quarter panel and roof sail panel that was used on the full-size 1968 Ford hardtops.

The four-door Landau models featured unique rear doors and tops. Rear doors were hinged at the back, opening in a "suicide" fashion reminiscent of some 1930s sedans. The four-door Landau also used different seats than two-door models. A full-width bench seat was used in place of bucket seats in the front, while in the back, the Landau used a regular bench seat rather than the curved, "coved" back seat used in the two-door cars.

Unique features weren't just limited to the four-door Landaus, however. The two-door Thunderbirds had an interesting way of dealing with their quarter windows. Rather than these windows lowering themselves into the rear quarter panel as on most cars, the two-door Thunderbird's rear quarter windows retracted into the roof C panel.

Production figures were up in 1967 over those recorded for 1966 models. One model missing from the 1967 tally was the convertible which was dropped at the end of the 1966 model year. In 1966, Ford had produced and sold only 5,049 Thunderbird convertibles. In marked contrast to that figure was the production figure for the new four-door Landau: 24,967. Ford was more than happy with the tradeoff between a model lost and a model gained.

1967

Standard Equipment
390ci 4-barrel V-8 315hp Thunderbird Special V-8
SelectShift Cruise-O-Matic transmission
Variable-speed windshield wipers
Windshield washers
Deluxe seat belts
Backup lights
Remote control outside rearview mirror
Tilt-Away steering wheel
Power brakes
Front disc brakes
Power steering
Retractable headlight covers
AM radio
Automatic parking brake release
Full wheel covers
Courtesy lights
Map light
Glove box light
Ashtray light
Luggage compartment light
Sequential turn signals
MagicAire heater and defroster
Undercoating
Comfort Stream ventilation system

Colors

Code	Name
T	Candyapple Red
V	Burnt Umber
6	Pebble Beige
A	Raven Black
M	Wimbledon White
X	Vintage Burgundy
C	Charcoal Gray
4	Silver Frost
K	Nightmist Blue
Q	Brittany Blue
F	Arcadian Blue
N	Diamond Blue
U	Lunar Green
B	Frost Turquoise
R	Ivy Green
Z	Sauterne Gold
H	Diamond Green
E	Beige Mist
2	Phoenician Yellow
P	Pewter Mist

Vinyl Top Colors
Black
Blue
Brown
Parchment

Optional Equipment

428ci V-8 345hp	$90.68
Power retracting antenna	$28.97
Six-way power driver's seat	$97.32
Power remote trunk lid release	$12.63
Power windows	$103.95
Limited slip differential	$46.69
Tinted windshield and windows	$47.49
Highway pilot control	$129.55
Convenience control panel, two-door	$77.73
Convenience control panel, four-door	$101.10
SelectAire air conditioner	$421.49
AM Radio/StereoSonic tape system	$128.49
AM/FM radio	$89.94
Reclining passenger seat and headrest	$57.08
AM/FM multiplex stereo radio with speakers	$163.77
Super-luxury cloth interior trim	$97.21
Leather and vinyl upholstery combination	$201.06
Two-tone paint	$25.25
Styled steel wheel covers	$35.70
Deluxe wheel covers	$19.48
Five whitewall tires with red bands	$51.98

A fastback roofline is the most prominent feature of this stylist's rendition of a 1967 Thunderbird.

1968

For 1968, Ford made few changes to the Thunderbird. For openers, the three Thunderbird models—hardtop, two-door and four-door Landau—were offered as bucket or bench seat models.

On the exterior, the front grille was changed, replacing the big Thunderbird emblem that had resided in the center with a smaller emblem attached to each retractable headlight door. Also new this year was the placement of cornering lamps and reflectors on the front fenders and reflectors on the rear quarter panels. The lower body trim was also considerably thinner.

As the 1968 model year began, the 315hp 390ci V-8 was still the standard Thunderbird powerplant, but after January 1, 1968, the 390 was dropped and the 428 became the standard powerplant. If that wasn't enough pow-

The 1968 Thunderbird featured a few changes from the 1967 model it replaced. This styling exercise featured some simulated fender vents that didn't make it to production.

1968

Code	Model
65A	Two-door hardtop with bucket seats
65B	Two-door Landau hardtop with bucket seats
65C	Two-door hardtop with bench seat
65D	Two-door Landau hardtop with bench seat
57B	Four-door Landau with bucket seats
57C	Four-door Landau with bench seat

Colors and Codes

E	Beige Mist
H	Diamond Green
J	Midnight Aqua
L	Silver Pearl
P	Pewter Mist
V	Alaska Blue
Z	Oxford Gray
A	Raven Black
B	Royal Maroon
I	Lime Gold
M	Wimbledon White
N	Diamond Blue
Q	Brittany Blue
R	Highland Green
T	Candyapple Red
U	Tahoe Turquoise
W	Meadowlark Yellow
X	Presidential Blue
X	Sunlit Gold
6	Pebble Beige

Prices

Two-door hardtop	$4,638.91
Two-door Landau	$4,768.36
Four-door Landau	$4,847.28

Optional Equipment

429ci Thunderjet V-8	$53.18
Power antenna (retracting)	$28.97
Six-way power driver's seat	$97.32
Bucket seats and console	$64.77
Power windows	$103.95
Tinted windows	$47.49
Highway pilot control (Tilt-Away steering wheel required)	$97.21
Tilt-Away steering wheel	$66.14
Front cornering lamps	$33.70
Convenience Group, two-door	$77.73
Convenience group, four-door	$101.10
SelectAire air conditioner	$427.07
SelectAire air conditioner with automatic temperature controls	$499.22
AM Radio/StereoSonic tape player	$128.49
Reclining passenger seat	$41.49
Brougham cloth interior	$162
For two-door bucket seats	$129.54
For four-door with bench seats	$161.98
Brougham leather and vinyl trim bucket seat interior	$194.31
Styled steel wheel covers	$35.70
Styled steel deluxe wheel covers	$57.08
Five whitewall tires	$43.12

Here we see a 1968 Thunderbird four-door Landau model with its rear "suicide" door in the open posi-tion. You don't see many of these at shows these days.

This Landau four-door styling exercise features a different roof treatment than that found on the 1968 production cars.

er, for $53.18 the Thunderbird buyer could opt for a 429ci Thunderjet V-8 rated at 360hp. The 428 was still rated at 345hp.

1969

Several changes were made to the 1969 Thunderbirds, making it somewhat easier to tell these cars from the 1967 and 1968 Thunderbirds.

The grille was once again changed, this time the die-cast grille featured a mesh pattern bisected by a dominant horizontal bar with three complimentary vertical bars. As in 1967, a new, stylized Thunderbird emblem was placed in the center of the grille. Just below the grille, a revised bumper was pared down and a body-colored splash pan was placed under it.

The size of the rear quarter panel reflector panel was reduced, compared to that which was used on the 1968 models, and the lower-body trim now sported a ribbed look. The

Here is another ad where Ford is promoting the 1969 Thunderbird sunroof option. The last time Ford had offered this item had been in 1960. *Jerry Bougher Ads*

A load of new 1969 Thunderbirds, including a four-door Landau, on their way to a new car dealer in 1969. Note the new Continental MK IIIs on the bottom and the vintage Ford "N" Series tractor pulling this trailer. *Dick Copello Collection*

Landau two-door model sported a wider roof C-panel that did away with the rear quarter windows. The regular two-door hardtop retained a roof with a narrower C panel and it still incorporated the use of small rear quarter windows.

The 1969 also received a new taillight treatment. The single, wide taillight used since 1966 was replaced by two taillights, each sporting a stylized Thunderbird emblem. The backup lights were incorporated behind a panel between the two taillights, and the name "Thunderbird" was spelled out across this panel.

On the inside, all Thunderbirds this year came equipped with headrests, simulated teakwood appliqué trim, and solid-state instrumentation.

In these two vintage 1969 Ford Public Relations photos, we see a 1969 two-door Landau and a close-up of the factory sunroof option. *Ford Motor Company*

The only engine listed for the 1968 Thunderbird was the 429 Thunderjet rated at 360hp.

For the first time since 1960, a factory sunroof option was made available for the Thunderbird. However, this new version was electrically operated rather than manual. This option was available on both two- and four-door versions of the Landau.

Despite all these refinements, production and sales were down this year, primarily due to increased competition in the personal/luxury car market. This competition came from a redesigned Pontiac Grand Prix, a sleek Buick Riviera, and Oldsmobile's Toronado. The

A Ford promotional postcard for the 1968 Thunderbird four-door Landau. *Ford Motor Company*

Thunderbird even lost sales to the new Continental Mark III, a car that was built on the same assembly line as the Thunderbird.

This styling proposal was probably for a 1969 or 1970 Thunderbird.

Rear 3/4 promotional photo shows the redesigned taillight and side-marker lights and the new wheel covers for 1968. *Ford Motor Company*

Although it's hard to discern in this photo, this 1969 Landau two-door hardtop is equipped with a factory sunroof. Optional sunroofs had not been available since 1960. *Ford Motor Company*

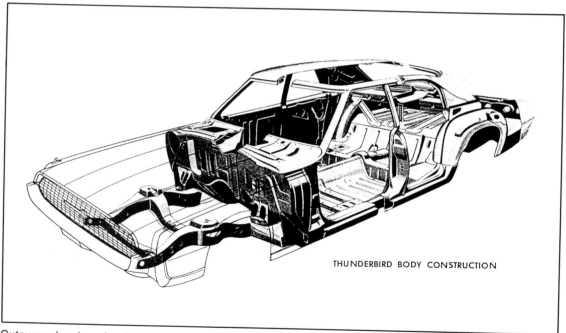

THUNDERBIRD BODY CONSTRUCTION

Cutaway drawing showing how a Thunderbird is constructed under its sheet metal skin. *Ford Motor Company*

1969

Standard Equipment
Automatic parking brake release
Power front disc brakes
429 Thunderjet V-8 engine
Super Diamond Luster enamel finish
Retractable headlights
Power steering
AM radio
Rear sequential turn signal indicators
Vinyl roofs on Landau models
Dual hydraulic braking system
Remote control driver's exterior rearview mirror
Energy-absorbing steering column and wheel
Reversible keys
MagicAire heater
Full wheel covers
Backup lights
Electric self-regulating clock
Flight bench seat
Power ventilation system
SelectShift Cruise-O-Matic transmission
8.45x15in four-ply rated black sidewall tires

Exterior Colors
A Raven Black
B Royal Maroon
C Black Jade
G Lilac Frost
H Diamond Green
I Lime Gold
J Midnight Aqua
K Midnight Orchid
M Wimbledon White
N Diamond Blue
Q Brittany Blue
R Morning Gold
S Champagne Gold
T Candyapple Red
U Tahoe Turquoise
V Copper Flame
W Meadowlark Yellow
X Presidential Blue
Y Indian Fire
Z Oxford Gray

Interior Combinations
Standard Vinyl (hardtop and Landau)
Black
White
Blue
Red
Nugget Gold
All-Vinyl Bucket Seats (hardtop and two-door Landau)
Black
Red
Blue
Ivy Gold
White/Nugget Gold
Brougham Luxury Cloth and Vinyl (Hardtop and Landau)
Black
Blue
Red (four-door only)
Ivy Gold
Nugget Gold
Brougham Luxury Cloth and Vinyl bucket seats (hardtop and Landau)
Black
Red (two-door only)
Blue
Nugget Gold
Brougham Leather Bucket Seats
Black
White

Vinyl Roof Colors :
Black
White
Dark Blue
Ivy Gold

Optional Equipment

Electric sunroof (Landaus only)	$453.30
Sure Track brake control system	$194.31
Flight bucket seats and console	$64.77
Reclining passenger seat	$41.49
Six-way power seat	$98.89
Power windows	$109.22
Power trunk lid release	$14.85
Power retracting antenna	$28.97
Rear defogger	$22.33
Electric defroster	$84.25
Tinted windows	$47.49
Highway pilot speed control	$97.21
Tilt-Away steering wheel	$66.14
Convenience Group, four-door	$101.10
Convenience Group, two-door	$77.73
SelectAire air conditioner	$427.07
Selectaire air conditioner (with automatic temperature controls)	$499.22
AM/FM stereo with speakers	$150.29
StereoSonic tape player with AM radio	$128.49
Dual rear speakers (standard with StereoSonic or AM/FM radios)	$33.07
Limited slip differential	$46.69
Four-note horn	$15.59
Brougham cloth and vinyl interior (full-width seat models)	$161.98
Brougham vinyl interior with leather seating surfaces (bucket seats only)	$194.31
Brougham cloth and vinyl interior (bucket seats)	$129.54
Deluxe seat belts with warning light	$15.59
Rear lamp outage indicator	$25.91
Supplemental brake lamps (four-doors only)	$33.70
Protection Group, two-door models	$25.28
Protection Group, four-door models	$29.17
Heavy-duty suspension	$27.99
Simulated styled steel wheel covers	$35.70
Deluxe wheel covers	$57.08
Five whitewall tires	$42.88
Five red band tires	$52.04
Five 215R15in radial ply WSW tires	$101.30

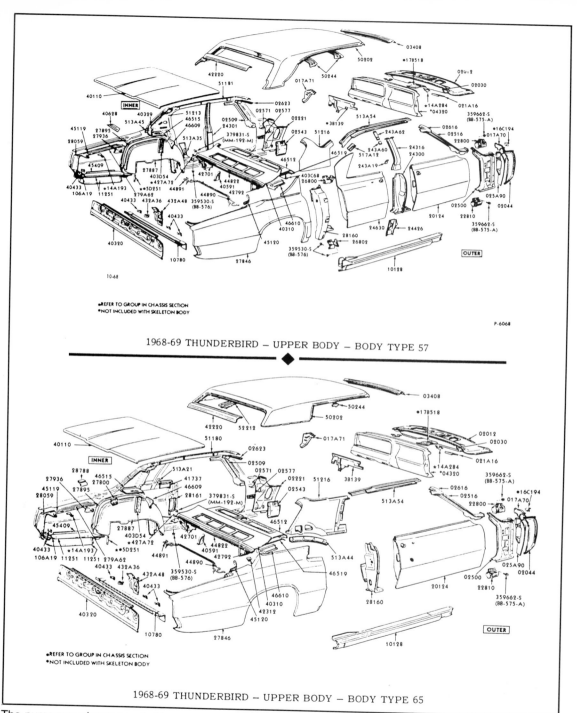

1968-69 THUNDERBIRD – UPPER BODY – BODY TYPE 57

1968-69 THUNDERBIRD – UPPER BODY – BODY TYPE 65

The numerous pieces needed to construct either a
two-door or four-door 1968–1969 Thunderbird.
Ford Motor Company

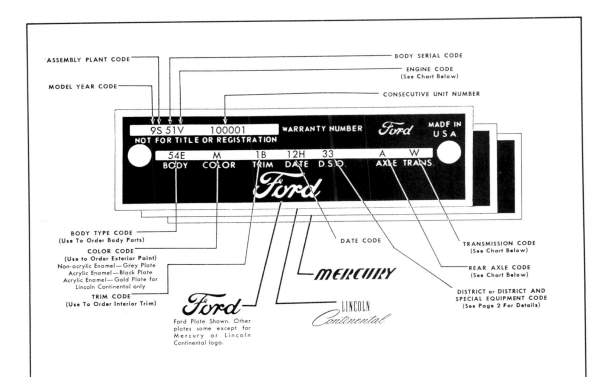

ENGINE CODES

CODE	CYL	CID	CARB VENTURI
A	8	460†	4V
B	6	240*	1V Police
D	8	302	2V Police & Taxi
E	6	240	1V Taxi
F	8	302	2V
H	8	351	2V
K	8	429	2V
L	6	250	1V
M	8	351	4V
N	8	429	4V
P	8	428	4V Police Interceptor
Q	8	428	4V Cobra Jet
R	8	428	4V Cobra Jet Ram Air
S	8	390	4V Improved Performance
T	6	200*	1V
U	6	170*	1V
V	6	240	1V
X	8	390†	2V Premium Fuel
Y	8	390	2V Regular Fuel

†L-M only
*Ford only

TRANSMISSION CODES

CODE	TRANSMISSION TYPE
	Manual
1	3 Speed
5	4 Speed Wide Ratio (2.78 1st Gear)
6	4 Speed Close Ratio (2.32 1st Gear)
	Automatic
U	C6 (XPL)
W	C4 (XP3)
X	Gruise-O-Matic (FMX)
Z	C6 (XPL Special)

REAR AXLE RATIO CODES

REGULAR	RATIO	LOCKING
F	2.35:1 (Mustang only)	—
2	2.75:1	K
3	2.79:1	—
4	2.80:1	M
5	2.83:1	—
6	3.00:1	Ø
C	3.08:1	U
7	3.10:1	—
8	3.20:1 (Falcon only)	Q
9	3.25:1	R
A	3.50:1	S
—	3.91:1	V
—	4.30:1	W

Compare this car identification plate used on all Ford products in 1969 to the patent plate used on earlier Thunderbirds. *Ford Motor Company*

Chapter 7

1970-1971: Bunkie Comes Calling and the Thunderbird Takes on GM Airs

★★★★★	1970 Thunderbird two-door Landau
★★★★	1970 Thunderbird two-door hardtop
★★★★	1970 Thunderbird four-door Landau
★★★★★	1971 Thunderbird two-door Landau
★★★★	1971 Thunderbird two-door hardtop
★★★★	1971 Thunderbird four-door Landau

The late Henry Ford II was always hunting for good automotive talent to bring into his company. One of his favorite hunting spots was General Motors. Although he brought in people from other companies too, he really relished luring away the General's best people. Henry bagged some good GM employees in the late-1940s and early-1950s when he was rebuilding Ford Motor Company, and he repeated those earlier days in 1968 when he grabbed one of GM's brightest stars, Semon E. "Bunkie" Knudsen.

Bunkie Knudsen had accomplished a lot during his twenty-year General Motors career. He had risen from an entry-level position to become one of GM's best vice-presidents in the 1960s. His biggest claim to fame was revitalizing the Pontiac Motor Division in

the late-1950s. Before Bunkie, Pontiac had the reputation of building cars for older people—cars that weren't necessarily exciting. Knudsen pushed to change the way Pontiacs looked and were perceived. He also pushed Pontiac into racing and made sure that the cars had powerful engines for street and highway use.

In the late-1960s, Knudsen had his eye on GM's presidential office, a position he believed he deserved based on his track record. The top brass evidently thought otherwise, and Bunkie was passed over a couple of times for the presidential chair.

Knudsen was disappointed at this turn of events and let his feelings be known. Detroit's automotive industry has quite a grapevine,

The four-door Landau was still available in 1970. Sales for this model were starting to fall off by then, but Ford kept it in the Thunderbird lineup for one more year. *Ford Motor Company*

and it didn't take long for this information to reach the penthouse at Ford's World Headquarters building. Shortly thereafter Ford and Knudsen met. An announcement followed that Knudsen had gotten his desired presidential chair—across town at Ford.

Neither Ford nor Knudsen felt in any way ashamed of their deal. Knudsen believed he had deserved the GM presidential promotion and that he had given the company more than a few chances to see things his way. Ford thought this "turnabout was fair play," because forty-five years earlier GM had lured Knudsen's father away from Ford. In short order, the elder Knudsen had turned a sickly Chevrolet into Ford's strongest competitor.

Not everyone at Ford rejoiced at Bunkie Knudsen's good fortune. One man in particular thought he deserved the presidential chair more than this outsider. His name was Lee Iacocca—an automotive guy cut from the same cloth as Knudsen. Both were "hands-on" managers with strong egos and personalities, and both had their supporters and detractors. The two factions quickly set about trying to outdo each other, which probably pleased Henry Ford II to no end.

When Bunkie arrived in February 1968, the design of the 1969 Thunderbird was "set in stone," so to speak, as production would begin in just a few months. Although he was too late to influence that model, Knudsen had more than enough time to add a few personal touches to the 1970 model.

This new-for-1970 Thunderbird ad shows a Landau two-door hardtop on the tarmac at an airport. Note the new Pan-Am 747s in the background.

Chief among the changes that Bunkie wrought was an aggressive, protruding, V'd front end like that associated with Pontiacs of the time. This protrusion was made by

This Thunderbird styling proposal dated 11-7-68 shows a heavy GM influence. At the time, former GM vice-president Bunkie Knudsen had been lured to Ford to serve as president. He may have had some input on this project.

This 1971 Thunderbird styling exercise shows a certain Pontiac influence in its pointed front end.

adding a header panel to the front end and by pushing the grille out to stand alone. The grille was then flanked by a set of dual headlights in their own separate pods.

Knudsen also had Ford stylists redo the front fenders, hood, bumper, and the associated brackets needed to hold the whole thing together. The 1970 Thunderbird's nose was much busier and more involved than its predecessors.

From the doors back, the body was the same as that used for the 1967–1969 cars. The roof of the four-door Landau was unchanged, but the design of the two-door roof was more streamlined especially in the C panel area. From some angles, the roof looked like it might have been lowered, but this could be an optical illusion.

The 1970 Thunderbirds also featured a new, full-width taillight design, redesigned cornering lamps and reflectors, side panel trim, and color-coordinated wheel covers.

When the redesigned Thunderbirds were shown to the dealers in the summer of 1969, some of them weren't too happy with the design revisions. The Thunderbird had been a trendsetter, "unique in all the world" as the Thunderbird brochures proudly stated, but now it looked like something you could buy at a Pontiac, Buick, or even a Chevrolet dealer.

Was Knudsen bothered by what dealers were saying about his car? If he was, he didn't

Some Thunderbird designs, like this 1971 model, bore a resemblance to General Motors cars of the period. The front end of this car looks like it was taken from a Pontiac, while the back end looks like a Buick Riviera.

This Ford Public Relations photo released in 1970 shows a nattily clad couple with their new 1971 Thunderbird two-door Landau. *Ford Motor Company*

show it; he just kept making changes on other Ford products. He was getting more powerful and making more demands—a situation not overlooked by Henry Ford, who started wondering whether Bunkie had his sights set on a loftier position. In plain talk, he had gotten too big for his britches, and in September 1969, soon after his "Bunkie Birds" hit the streets, Ford unceremoniously showed Knudsen the door. His reign at Ford had lasted about eighteen months, and the man chosen to take his place was none other than Lee Iacocca.

1970

Exterior Colors and Codes

(A) Black
(B) Dark Maroon
(C) Dark Ivy Green Metallic
(E) Light Blue
(F) Dark Aqua Metallic
(J) Bright Blue Metallic
(L) Light Gray Metallic
(M) White
(P) Medium Ivy Green Metallic
(Q) Medium Blue Metallic
(R) Dark Brown Metallic
(S) Nugget Gold Metallic
(T) Red
(X) Dark Blue
(Y) Chestnut Metallic
(Z) Dark Slate Gray Metallic
(2) Light Ivy Yellow
(5) Ginger Metallic
(8) Light Gold
(9) Yellow
(19) Ivy Bronze Metallic
(09) Olive Bronze Metallic
(59) Medium Red Metallic
(89) Fall Bronze Metallic

Options

SelectAire air conditioner (manual controls)	$427
SelectAire air conditioner (auto controls)	$499
Sure Track braking system	$194
Rear window defogger	$26
Emission control system (required in California)	$37
Tinted glass	$48
Power remote trunk lid release	$14
Power seat six-way full width	$99
Power seat six-way driver only	$99
Power seat six-way driver and passenger	$198
Power side windows	$110
AM/FM stereo radio and speakers	$150
High-back bucket seats and console	$78
Manual reclining passenger seat	$41
Split-bench seat (available only on four-door Landau with Brougham interior)	$78
Tilt-Away steering wheel	$52
StereoSonic tape system (AM radio)	$150
Power-operated sunroof (Landau models only)	$453
215R15in radial ply whitewall tires (standard with special Brougham option)	$30

Brougham Interior Trim Packages

Brougham cloth and vinyl bench and split-bench seats	$162
Brougham vinyl and leather surfaces on split-bench and high-back bucket seats	$227
Deluxe wheel covers	$52

This factory promotional postcard shows the new 1971 Thunderbird two-door Landau. *Robert Lucero Collection*

A 1971 Thunderbird hardtop in excellent, original condition awaits its turn on the auction block in 1992.

1971

During his tenure, Knudsen spared no expense when redoing Ford's cars. Consequently, little money remained after he left for updating the 1971 Thunderbirds. The front bumper, grille, and wheel covers were redesigned, and some updates were also made to the trim and equipment. Iacocca had to be satisfied with the Bunkie Bird for 1971, but he would have more money behind him to reshape the 1972 Thunderbird.

1971			
Exterior Colors and Codes		(C9)	Burgundy Fire
		(E9)	Green Fire (optional)
(A)	Black	(B9)	Walnut Fire
(M)	White	(H)	Light Green
(T)	Red	(P)	Medium Green Metallic
(B)	Maroon Metallic	(G)	Dark Green
(K)	Dark Gray Metallic	(S)	Gray Gold Metallic
(N)	Pastel Blue	(W)	Yellow
(Q)	Medium Blue Metallic	(O)	Light Yellow Gold
(X)	Dark Blue Metallic	(2)	Tan
(F)	Bright Aqua Metallic	(V)	Light Pewter Metallic
(D9)	Blue Fire	(R)	Dark Brown Metallic
		(5)	Medium Brown Metallic

Check out this styling mockup for a 1971 Thunderbird. Did you notice the two different headlight treatments?

Chapter 8

1972-1976: Thunderbirds on a Continental Scale

★★★★	1972 Thunderbird hardtop with sunroof
★★★	1972 Thunderbird hardtop
★★★★	1973 Thunderbird hardtop with sunroof
★★★	1973 Thunderbird hardtop
★★★★	1974 Thunderbird hardtop with sunroof
★★★★	1974 Thunderbird hardtop with moonroof
★★★	1974 Thunderbird hardtop
★★★★	1975 Thunderbird 20th Anniversary Copper Group
★★★★	1975 Thunderbird 20th Anniversary Silver Group
★★★★	1975 Thunderbird hardtop with sunroof
★★★★	1975 Thunderbird hardtop with moonroof
★★★	1975 Thunderbird hardtop
★★★★★★	1976 Thunderbird Creme and Gold Group
★★★★	1976 Thunderbird Lipstick Group
★★★★	1976 Thunderbird Bordeaux Group
★★★★	1976 Thunderbird hardtop with sunroof
★★★★	1976 Thunderbird hardtop with moonroof
★★★	1976 Thunderbird hardtop

With Bunkie out of the way, Lee Iacocca could get back to building the type of cars he wanted without fear of being criticized by an outsider. In the early 1970s, Iacocca was a proponent of "bigger is always better." For him, a better Thunderbird was a bigger Thunderbird. Make it heavier and load it down with the latest in comfort and convenience items, throw in some luxury touches, and voila, a new flagship was created. And for the Ford Division in 1972, the flagship of the entire line was going to be the new Thunderbird.

Most car enthusiasts know Iacocca was one of the driving forces behind the Mustang. What they may not know is that he was also the driving force behind the revival of the Continental Mark Series. It was Iacocca who during the mid-1960s spearheaded the move

Though this photo looks like a 1972 Ford LTD, the Thunderbird crest on the roof panel suggests that at one time this design was considered for the 1972 Thunderbird.

This Ford factory promotional photo shows a new 1972 Thunderbird Landau with a 1955 and a 1958 model in the background. *Ford Motor Company*

The Thunderbird Feeling. Only when you drive one can you truly experience it.

A great deal of that feeling comes from what we call "The Thunderbird Ride."

The ride comes from Thunderbird's new body/frame construction that helps absorb road shock and vibration. And a new suspension that's electronically tuned to the steel-belted radial tires for quiet, smooth road performance.

Another part of the feeling comes from Thunderbird's luxurious interior appointments—the enveloping comfort of its seats, the lush, cut-pile carpeting underfoot, and the increased roominess made possible by a longer wheelbase. They're all part of this magnificent personal automobile.

But there's really only one sure way to get the feeling of Thunderbird. Drive it. At your Ford Dealer's now.

A magazine ad for the 1972 Thunderbird.

to get the Continental Mark III cars into Lincoln showrooms by the end of the decade. The Continental Mark III was a very fine car, but it was expensive to build and not enough cars were sold for it to be a profit-maker.

Introduced in 1968, the Continental Mark III remained virtually unchanged through 1971. Iacocca knew he would have to make some changes to the car to retain, if not increase, its customer base. But making all the changes he thought were necessary would cost a lot of money, money that would take considerable time to recoup. However, if some of the costs to develop this new car could be shared by another model, that time could be greatly decreased.

The new Continental Mark package called for a coupe with a long hood and a short deck, a design also possessed by the Thunderbird (except for the four-door Landau). As the Thunderbird was ready for a design change, why not combine the two on the same platform? When the two luxury cars debuted as new 1972 models in the fall of 1971, American buyers saw a Continental and a Continental clone. Both the Thunderbird and Continental Mark IV were larger and heavier than their 1971 counterparts, thus fitting Iacocca's "bigger is better" maxim.

Although the new Thunderbird and Continental Mark IV shared the same platform and body components, there were enough differences in trim and body stampings to easily differentiate the two. The Thunderbird's bumpers, headlights, grille, taillights, wheel covers, and dress-up trim were different from those of the Mark IV. The front fenders and rear quarter panels on both cars looked similar, but the wheelwell lips were more pronounced on the Continental, its decklid stamping included a fake spare tire hump, and its roof stamping included a

cutout for an opera window, a feature the Thunderbirds wouldn't see until 1973.

The base engine for the Thunderbird was still the 429, but the Lincoln 460ci V-8, base powerplant for all Lincolns in 1972, was offered as an extra cost option.

This new Thunderbird was only available as one model: a two-door hardtop. The two- and four-door Landaus were a thing of the past. Now if you wanted to make your Thunderbird look different from another, you had to load it with accessories selected from a long list, one of which was the Glamour Paint Option, which offered the following paint colors: Blue Fire, Green Fire, Walnut Fire, Gold Fire, Copper Fire, Burgundy Fire, Lime Fire, and Cinnamon Fire. These colors were called Glamour Paints because of their deep luster and an iridescent brilliancy that set them

In 1974, Ford brought out a special Thunderbird called the Burgundy Special Edition. This is one of the magazine ads used to promote it. *Jerry Bougher Ads*

The model in this ad seems to be beckoning us to join her for a ride in this new 1975 Thunderbird. *Jerry Bougher Ads*

Thunderbird interiors don't come any richer or more luxurious than the leather version that appeared in this 1976 Creme and Gold Special Edition Thunderbird.

1972

Options

Power-operated sunroof
Power windows
Power lock Group
Power antenna
SelectAire air conditioner (with automatic temperature controls)
Six-way full-width power seat
Six-way driver only power seat
Six-way driver and passenger power bucket seats
Tinted glass
Tilt-Away steering wheel
Fingertip speed control
Rim blow deluxe three-spoke steering wheel
Sure Track brake control system
Outside left-hand remote control mirror
Convenience light Group
Turnpike convenience Group
Deluxe seat and shoulder belts
Intermittent windshield wipers
Front cornering lights
Rear window electric defroster
AM/FM stereo radio
StereoSonic tape system (AM radio)
Vinyl roof
Dual rear seat speakers
Bumper guards
Bodyside protective molding
Glamour Paint option Group
Leather trim
Protection Group
Rocker panel moldings
Automatic seat back release
460 V-8 (air conditioner mandatory)
Split-bench seat
High-back split-bench seat
Manual reclining passenger seat
High-back bucket seats and console
Traction-Lok differential
Heavy-duty suspension Deluxe wheel covers

apart from the quieter, more subdued colors offered as standard choices. Ordering the Glamour Paint option also got the buyer color-keyed wheel covers, hood and bodyside pin striping, and tooled, silver Landau "S" bar inserts when a vinyl roof covering was ordered.

A Thunderbird milestone was reached during the 1972 model year, with the assembly of the one-millionth Thunderbird. This special model featured a unique gold finish; a white vinyl top; gold, color-keyed wheel covers; and a gold-tone grille. It was decorated with three special commemorative "Millionth Thunderbird" emblems: one in the center of each roof Landau iron and one installed on the right-hand side of the dashboard.

This car was loaned to a member of the Classic Thunderbird Club for one year. Sometime during 1973, George Watts, who owns the earliest 1955 Thunderbird still in existence, purchased this car from Ford for his personal collection. The commemorative Thunderbird was almost 1500lb heavier than Watts' 1955 Thunderbird and had grown in length from the 1955's 175.3in to 214in. The Thunderbird was no longer a personal car with a sporty flavor, it was now a luxury car

much closer in definition to the Lincoln than to the early Thunderbirds.

In 1972, Ford started producing Thunderbirds in its Los Angeles plant in addition to the Wixom plant. The Los Angeles plant built cars for the western United States, as well as Hawaii and Alaska. Cars built in Wixom were identified with a "Y" assembly plant code on their data plates, while cars produced in Los Angeles were marked with a "J" code.

How did the American public react to this more luxurious Thunderbird? With their wallets! Sales were up to 57,814 vehicles in 1972, more than 20,000 units higher than in 1971.

1973

The Thunderbird was primarily refined in 1973, with changes done mostly to the trim. Up front the Thunderbird featured a new "egg crate"-styled grille in place of the horizontal bar unit used in 1972. The grille was still flanked by dual headlights, but instead of being grouped together in one pod, the 1973 headlights were in individual pods. Above the grille on the header panel, the Thunderbird crest was replaced by the name "Thunderbird" spelled out in block letters, and a stylized Thunderbird crest hood ornament was installed above the panel. The 1973 and later Thunderbirds also came with a new federally mandated 5mph crash-resistant front bumper, which added quite a bit of weight to the front end. Restyled protective bodyside molding was installed this year; the wheel covers were redone, and an opera window option became available for those who wanted their Thunderbirds to look like the Continental Mark IV. These opera windows also provided a little more visibility on the car's right-hand side—a welcome relief from the large blind spot created by the massive C panels on these cars. After June 11, 1973, opera windows became standard equipment, as did power windows, tinted glass, a vinyl roof,

This ritzy-looking ad was used to promote the then-new Creme and Gold Special Edition Thunderbird. *Jerry Bougher Ads*

The 1976 Ford Thunderbird was indeed the last of a breed. These were the largest, heaviest, and most luxurious Thunderbirds ever to come out of Dearborn. *Ford Motor Company*

and automatic seat back releases. The opera windows were a popular accessory on the Thunderbird in 1973 and it's hard to find a car today that didn't come with them in 1973.

Other standard equipment found on the 1973 Thunderbird that was optional on other cars in its class included front bumper guards, steel-belted radial whitewall tires, impact-re-

1973

Standard Equipment
Steel door guard rails
Front bumper guards
Body molding with vinyl insert
Bright window moldings
Remote control left-hand outside mirror
Wheel covers
Individually adjustable split-bench seat
Aurora cloth seat trim with vinyl facings
Cut pile carpeting
Deluxe armrests
Interior courtesy lights
Energy-absorbing steering wheel
429ci V-8
SelectShift Cruise-O-Matic transmission
Steel-belted radial tires
Power front disc brakes
Power ventilation system
80amp battery
Inside hood lock release
Constant ratio power steering
AM radio
MagicAire heater and defroster
Electric clock
Full wheel covers
Spare tire lock
Energy-absorbing bumpers

These Items Came Standard on the Thunderbird After June 11, 1973:
Opera windows
Power windows
Tinted glass
Vinyl roof
Automatic seat back releases

Interior Colors
Standard bench seat with cloth and vinyl combination:
Black
Dark Green
Gold
Ginger
Tobacco
Dark Blue
Optional leather with vinyl trim:
Black
Tobacco
White
Dark Green
Optional bucket seat cloth and vinyl:
Black
Dark Green
Ginger
Dark Blue
Optional all-vinyl trim (bench seat):
Black
White
Dark Green
Gold
Ginger
Tobacco
Dark Blue

Vinyl Roof Colors
Cayman Grain:
Black
White
Dark Blue
Dark Green
Dark Brown
Beige
Gold
Light Blue
Odense Grain (exterior decor option only):
Copper
White
Blue
Green
Brown

Exterior Colors and Codes
(3A)	Pastel Blue
(3G)	Dark Blue Metallic
(4S)	Light Green
(6L)	Medium Gold Metallic
(1A)	Light Gray Metallic
(1C)	Black
(2J)	Maroon
(3D)	Medium Blue Metallic
(4P)	Medium Green Metallic
(4Q)	Dark Green Metallic
(5L)	Tan
(6B)	Light Yellow Gold
(6D)	Yellow
(5F)	Dark Brown Metallic
(9A)	White
(3L)	Silver Blue Fire
(4U)	Emerald Fire
(5K)	Almond Fire
(5P)	Mahogany Fire
(2G)	Burgundy Fire
(4D)	Green Fire
(5D)	Cinnamon Fire
(6G)	Gold Fire

(Fire colors were optional.)

sistant steel door guard beams, an inside hood release, cut pile carpeting, a MagicAire heater and defroster, a power ventilation system, and a spare tire lock.

Production shot up to 87,269 cars for the model year, which was quite a boost over the 1972 figures.

1974

The year 1974 would be mostly a stand pat year for the Thunderbird, with hardly any discernible differences between the 1973 and 1974 models.

One change that wasn't noticeable from the outside involved the powerplant. The 460ci V-8 was now the only engine offered in the Thunderbird. The 429 was dropped because it wasn't considered powerful enough to move the Thunderbird's extra weight around. Between 1973 and 1974, the Thunderbird gained an extra 300lb.

Also hard to see was the addition of a seat belt interlock system, a device mandated by Congress to force people to wear seatbelts. This annoying device made it impossible to start the car without first buckling the driver's seat belt. The interlock was so unpopular that Congress repealed the law after getting numerous complaints from its constituents. While the law was in effect, most people simply circumvented the system so that they

Ford promotional photograph of the 1972 Thunderbird. *Ford Motor Company*

could start their cars. To people accustomed to wearing seat belts, the interlock was a minor irritant, but for people who weren't going to be forced into wearing them, it constituted a major governmental intrusion. Needless to say, the devices didn't reappear after 1974.

Before we leave 1974 behind, some mention should be made of an action that was tak-

This studio photo of a 1973 Thunderbird shows a new feature that would be seen on most Thunderbirds for the next decade: the opera window. These windows helped alleviate the blind spot caused by the thick rear "C" pillars. *Ford Motor Company*

1974

Options

California emission controls	$20
Sure Track braking system	$189.05
Power antenna	$30.17
Power Lock Group	$59.45
Six-way driver power seat	$101.34
Six-way driver and passenger power bucket seats	$201.67
Power mini-vent windows	$67
Convenience Group	$51
SelectAire air conditioner (automatic temperature controls)	$70.73
Front cornering lamps	$35.66
Electric rear window defroster	$81.91
Glass moonroof	$767
Light Group	$125
Quick defrost windshield/rear window	$303
AM/FM stereo with speakers	$146.14
AM/FM stereo with tape player	$299
Manual reclining passenger bucket seat	$40
Fingertip speed control	$103.14
Deluxe three-spoke rim blow steering wheel	$37.99
Tilt-Away steering wheel	$50.74
Power-operated sunroof	$504.80
Turnpike Group	$132.51
Traction-Lok differential	$47.71
Dual exhausts	$51
Heavy-duty suspension	$27.26
Class III trailer-towing package	$45.82
Anti-theft alarm system	$76
Deluxe Bumper Group	$49
Exterior decor package	$135.23
Luggage compartment trim	$55
Fire Paint	$126
Starfire Paint	$165
Paint stripes	$17
Protection Group	$72
Protection Group on exterior decor package option	$65.18
Space saver spare tire	$74
Leather trim	$63.35
Picardy cloth velour trim	$61
Super Soft vinyl trim	$34
Color-keyed wheel covers (available with Fire and Starfire Paints)	$19
Deluxe wheel covers	$61.82
Simulated wire wheel covers	$82

en that would have a profound effect on the automotive business for many years to come: the first Arab Oil Embargo. When the Arabs shut off our oil supply in the fall of 1973, we faced gasless days and long lines at gas stations to purchase limited quantities of gasoline. An uncertain future for petroleum supplies certainly affected sales of cars like the Thunderbird. In fact, Thunderbird production dropped by almost 30,000 units from 1973. That decline prompted U.S. auto manufacturers to consider that maybe the day of "bigger is better" automobiles in the United States was ending.

1975

More luxury was the theme for the twentieth model year of the Thunderbird, which was introduced to the public on September 27, 1974. Ford promoted this more luxurious theme by pointing out that the Thunderbird came standard with many accessories that were extra cost options on other cars. Thunderbird buyers didn't have to pay extra for such items as a full vinyl roof, AM/FM stereo radio, SelectAire air conditioner (with manual controls), opera windows, burled walnut trim appliqués, power windows, 24oz cut pile car-

peting, 460ci V-8 with solid-state ignition system, whitewall steel-belted radial tires, and front disc brakes.

Discriminating Thunderbird buyers who sought a little more pampering in 1975 could opt for one or two special twentieth anniversary Thunderbird packages.

The first version was referred to as the Copper Luxury Group. If you chose this one, your Thunderbird was painted Copper Starfire or white. A copper-colored, fully padded vinyl half-roof with color-keyed copper window moldings complemented the paint scheme unless you ordered the optional moonroof. In that case, the vinyl half-roof was replaced by a full one. In addition to the special roof and paint, color-keyed bodyside moldings were installed to protect the car from parking lot damage. The opera windows on cars equipped with this package featured a gold-toned Thunderbird emblem. Further exterior glitter came via a set of cast-aluminum wheels and thin pinstriping on the hood and upper body.

On the inside, Copper Luxury Group cars had seats upholstered in either a copper-colored soft velour cloth or copper-colored leather. The dashboard, door panels, headlin-

1975

Color Choices and Codes

(1C)   Black
(9D)   Polar White
(3G)   Dark Blue Metallic
(3Q)   Pastel Blue
(4V)   Dark Yellow Green Metallic
(4Z)   Light Green Gold Metallic
(47)   Light Green
(5Q)   Dark Brown Metallic
(6N)   Medium Ivy Yellow
(2M)   Dark Red
(6Q)   Dark Gold Metallic
(3P)   Blue Starfire
(51)   Cinnamon Starfire
(2G)   Medium Red Metallic Starfire
(1J)   Silver Starfire
(3R)   Silver Blue Starfire
(41)   Emerald Starfire
(54)   Bronze Starfire
(52)   Copper Starfire

Note: Starfire Paints were optional.

Options

Four-wheel disc brakes
Sure Track braking system
Traction-Lok differential
Front cornering lamps
Dual-exhaust system
Fingertip speed control
Heavy-duty suspension
Class III towing package
Low-vacuum warning light
Optional axle ratio
AM/FM radio stereo with tape player
SelectAire air conditioner (automatic temperature controls)
Electric rear window defroster
Power-operated glass moonroof
Power-operated sunroof
Power antenna
Six-way power driver seat
Six-way power passenger seat
Power Mini-vent windows
Reclining passenger seat
Space saver spare tire
Tilt-Away steering wheel
Super Soft vinyl seat trim
Quick Defrost windshield and rear window
Copper Luxury Group
Silver Luxury Group
Convenience Group
Light Group
Power Lock Group
Protection Group
Turnpike Group
Wide body molding
Anti-theft alarm system
Deep-dish cast-aluminum wheels
Starfire Paint finishes
Dual body and hood pinstripes
Leather seat trim
Pictor velour cloth seat trim
Deluxe wheel covers
Simulated wire wheel covers
Wide-band whitewall radial tires

er, and carpet were also copper-colored, and copper-colored deluxe trim and carpeting adorned the trunk.

If copper wasn't your personal choice in a special model Thunderbird, Ford also offered a Silver Luxury Group package. This car was painted Silver Starfire and came with a silver-colored vinyl half-roof. If a moonroof was specified, the roof became full vinyl. These cars also came equipped with color-coordinated wide bodyside moldings and deluxe wire wheel covers. The Thunderbird crest in the opera windows was done in a silver-tone finish.

Interiors were available in either silver or red. Seat coverings for both colors were available in either a soft velour or leather. The trunk was trimmed in a silver color.

Even with all this extra Thunderbird 20th Anniversary hoopla, Ford couldn't reverse the trend of declining Thunderbird sales. It was evident that the Thunderbird needed a new direction—and Ford designers, engineers, and product planners were well on their way to creating that new Thunderbird. But the old Thunderbird would have to soldier on for one more year until the new Thunderbird was ready to test its wings.

1976

Ford pulled out all the stops to produce the biggest and most luxurious Thunderbirds ever for the 1976 model year. This would be the last model year for this large "Luxocruiser" Thunderbird. The last of a dying breed, the 1976 Thunderbird would be the biggest and most opulent T-Bird of all time.

In 1975, Ford had offered two 20th Anniversary Thunderbird packages; for those who wanted a special car. In 1976, it offered

Rear 3/4 shot shows off the 1974 Thunderbird's taillights, side molding trim, wheel covers, and back window. *Ford Motor Company*

three Luxury Packages: the Creme and Gold Luxury Group, the Bordeaux Luxury Group, and the Lipstick Luxury Group. The Creme and Gold version had to be the most ostentatious of the trio. The sides of its creme-colored hood, top, and trunk lid were highlighted by Gold Starfire paint. This two-tone combo was

hard to miss: a car definitely not for introverts.

For those who wanted the look of understated elegance, the deep red color of the Bordeaux package was more appropriate. The target audience for the Lipstick Luxury Group is not quite clear. By the name, you

The "Silver Anniversary Edition" Thunderbird was offered in 1975. It featured silver paint, color coordi-

nated side moldings, and a silver vinyl top. *Ford Motor Company* would think that this model was meant to appeal to women, but it's likely just as many were sold to men because its shade of red gave the car a very sporty flair. Regardless which package a 1976 buyer chose, these luxury options added about $700 to the base price of a 1976 Thunderbird.

Even without the special Luxury Packages, the 1976 Thunderbird was still a neat car if you were looking for a personal luxury vehicle in the mid-1970s. Once again, the Thunderbird featured many luxurious accessories as standard equipment, including a 460ci V-8 coupled to the best automatic transmission in the business, power steering, power disc brakes, power windows, and power ventilation. Other luxury touches included the burled walnut trim appliqués, Aurora cloth and vinyl seat coverings, deluxe door panels, 24oz cut pile carpeting, and courtesy lighting fixtures. The Thunderbird in standard form was one loaded automobile. And if you wanted an even more luxurious Thunderbird, Ford had a long list of options.

The 1976 Thunderbirds were fine cars in their own right, but the time had come for them to take on a new image, an image more in tune with the needs of late-1970s society. The Thunderbirds that would follow these last of the Luxocruisers were smaller, more agile, lighter, and more performance-oriented. They'll never be more luxurious, though, because as far as luxury goes in a Thunderbird package, the epitome was reached in 1976.

1976

Bordeaux Luxury Package
Bordeaux Starfire finish (Code 25)
Dark Red or Silver Odense vinyl half-roof
Color-keyed border moldings
Color-keyed wide body moldings
Dual Body and hood pinstripes
Wire wheel covers
Rich leather seat appointments (Code RD) or plush
  red media velour cloth (Code QD)
Color-keyed interior components
Color-keyed 24oz cut pile carpeting
Luggage compartment dress-up

Lipstick Luxury Package
Lipstick Red finish (Code 2U)
Bright Red Odense grain vinyl half-roof
Color-keyed border moldings
Color-keyed wide body moldings
Dual body and hood pinstripes
Wire wheel covers
White leather seating appointments (Code KN)
  or White Super Soft vinyl appointments (Code JN)
Red and white door trim panels
Color-keyed interior components
Color-keyed 24oz cut pile carpeting
Color-keyed luggage compartment trim

Creme and Gold Luxury Group
Gold Starfire finish on body
Creme (Off-white) finish on hood, roof, and decklid
Unique tape stripes at beltline
Gold Odense grain vinyl half-roof
Color-keyed border moldings
Deep-dish cast-aluminum wheels
Gold Opera window Thunderbird crest
Creme wide body moldings

Creme and Gold leather seat coverings or Plus Gold
  media velour cloth
Gold instrument panel appliqué
Color-keyed 24oz cut pile carpeting
Luggage compartment dress-up

Standard Features
460ci V-8
Solid-state ignition
SelectShift Cruise-O-Matic transmission
Power steering
Power front disc brakes
SelectAire air conditioner (manual temperature
  controls)
Automatic parking brake release
AM radio (dual front door-mounted speakers)
Power windows
61amp battery and alternator
Burled walnut interior trim appliqués
Inside hood release
Power ventilation system
Courtesy lighting
Individually adjustable split-bench front seat
Full wheel covers
Aurora cloth and vinyl seat coverings
Electric clock
24oz cut pile carpeting
Color-keyed deluxe seat belts
Thunderbird sound package
Odense vinyl roof covering
Opera windows with Thunderbird insignias
Remote control left-hand exterior mirror
Stand-up hood ornament
Bright moldings
Steel-belted black sidewall radial tires
Vinyl insert body moldings
Deluxe Bumper Group

Option Prices (as of March 26, 1976)

Base Price 1976 Thunderbird two-door hardtop	$7,790
SelectAire air conditioner with automatic temperature controls	$88
Power antenna	$39
Anti-theft alarm system	$84
Optional rear axle ratio (3:1)	$14
Traction-Lok differential	$55
Four-wheel disc brakes	$184
Sure Tack braking system	$378
Convenience Group	$84
Front cornering lamps	$43
Electric rear window defroster	$99
Electric Quick Defrost windshield and rear window	$355
California emission control system	$50
Dual exhaust	$72
Tinted glass	$66
High-altitude option	$13
Fuel system monitoring light	$20
Light Group	$164
Power locks	$86
Security Lock Group	$18
Luggage compartment dress-up	$59
Bordeaux Luxury Group (velour cloth interior)	$624
Bordeaux Luxury Group (leather seat trim)	$700
Creme and Gold Luxury Group (velour seat trim)	$717
Creme and Gold Luxury Group (leather seat trim)	$793
Lipstick Luxury Group (vinyl seat trim)	$337
Lipstick Luxury Group (leather seat trim)	$546
Driver's side illuminated vanity mirror	$43
Wide color-keyed vinyl insert body molding (standard on Luxury Groups)	$121
Power moonroof	$879
Starfire Paint finish	$204
Protection Group	$87
AM/FM stereo radio	$145
AM/FM stereo search radio	$296
Quadrasonic tape player AM/FM radio	$382
Tape player AM/FM stereo radio	$249
Manual reclining passenger bucket seat	$70
Automatic seat back release	$30
Power seat six-way driver only	$132
Power seat six-way driver and passenger bucket seats	$250
Power lumbar support seat (requires optional power seat)	$86
Fingertip speed control	$120
Tilt-Away steering wheel	$68
Dual body and hood pinstripes (standard with Bordeaux and Lipstick Groups)	$33
Power sunroof	$716
Heavy-duty suspension	$29
Space saver spare tire	$86
Heavy-duty trailer-towing package	$92
Kasman cloth trim	$96
Leather trim (standard with Luxury Groups)	$239
Super Soft vinyl seat trim	$55
Turnpike Group (consists of fingertip speed control, manual reclining passenger seat, and trip odometer)	$180
Power mini-vent windows	$79
Deluxe wheel covers	$67
Simulated wire wheel covers (standard on Bordeaux and Lipstick Luxury Groups)	$88
Simulated wire wheel covers (on Creme and Gold cars $163 credit)	
Deep-dish cast-aluminum wheels (standard on Creme and Gold) Bordeaux or Lipstick Luxury cars	$163
All others	$251
Tires: Five JR7 8x15 WSW steel-belted radial	$41
Five LR7 8x15 wide-band WSW steel-belted radials	$59

Chapter 9

1977-1979: Downsizing and Lower Prices Equal More Sales

The seventh series of Thunderbirds went through quite a metamorphosis. Released in the fall of 1976, they had lost some 700-900lb of fat and 10in of length. They were also more fun to drive.

They no longer shared the body and bulk of the Continental Mark IV, but were now on a trimmed down, mid-size platform Ford called the LTD II. This platform replaced the old Torino/Fairlane models and, in addition to the Thunderbird and Cougar, could accommodate two- and four-door coupe and sedan bodies, station wagons, and the Ranchero. Sharing a platform and body components doesn't work well all the time, but by using different roof treatments to make each series look different, Ford was successful with this program.

Evolution of a classic. This photo was sent out by Ford's Public Affairs Division in 1977 and shows 1955, 1958, and 1965 models, as well as the new 1977. *Ford Motor Company*

Ford was looking to downsize the Thunderbird in the mid-1970s, and this proposal shows a roofline on a smaller car platform that looks like the roofline used on the Ford Fairmont Futura.

What worked well for the Thunderbird was a two-door coupe roof with a unique wrap-over band, targa style, that went from one side of the body to the other. Ford had used a similar treatment in the 1950s with the Fairlane Crown Victoria hardtops. Back then, such a band served no other function than to enhance the appearance, but with the 1977 Thunderbird body, it helped reinforce the body by adding some structural rigidity without extra bulk. This wraparound "B" pillar also made a nice separation piece between the door windows and the new, large rear quarter windows (which afforded greater visibility). Ford also included a set of opera windows on the Thunderbird, a luxury car staple since the early-1970s. The opera windows were in a vertical plane now, rather than a horizontal plane, and were narrow enough to find a home in the Thunderbird's wraparound roof bar.

Ford's 1977 Thunderbird was available in two models: the base two-door hardtop model and the upscale deluxe Town Landau model. The standard powerplant for the 1977 Thunderbird was a 302ci 2-barrel V-8, unless the car was destined for California or a high-altitude area. Then the base engine was Ford's 351ci 2-barrel V-8. If that wasn't enough, Ford offered two optional 400ci V-8s, one a 2-barrel model and the other a 4-barrel. The Thunderbird also came equipped with power steering, power front disc brakes, SelectShift Cruise-O-Matic transmission, an AM radio, an electric

In the late 1970s, Ford was looking to Europe for design input that could be used on its domestic products. Ford even purchased the House of Ghia in Italy to help them work on designs. This car wears a Ghia license plate indicating that Ghia or its designers worked on the project.

clock, color-keyed cut pile carpeting, concealed headlamps, solid-state ignition, and a host of other standard features—all in a very good-looking car for about $5,063 in base model form.

For customers who didn't mind spending more money for some extra pampering, Ford offered the deluxe Town Landau model at a base price of $7,990. For that extra money, the buyer received a brushed-aluminum roof wraparound appliqué, turbine-style cast-aluminum wheels, 18oz cut pile carpeting, air conditioning, dual sport mirrors, AM/FM stereo search radio, 400ci V-8, power locks, Tilt-Away steering wheel, power windows,

This factory promotional postcard of a new 1977 Thunderbird coupe was sent to Paul C. McLaughlin by his grandfather, who was selling new Fords in 1976. *Ford Motor Company*

1977

Colors and Codes

(1C)	Black
(1G)	Silver Metallic
(2M)	Dark Red
(2U)	Lipstick Red
(3G)	Dark Blue Metallic
(3V)	Bright Blue Glow
(46)	Dark Jade Metallic
(5Q)	Dark Brown Metallic
(6P)	Creme
(7L)	Light Jade Glow
(9D)	Polar White
(1N)	Dove Gray
(8Y)	Champagne Metallic
(8K)	Bright Saddle Metallic
(2Y)	Rose Glow
(8W)	Chamois Glow
(1P)	Medium Gray Metallic (two-tone paint only)
(86)	Pastel Beige (Town Landau only)

Vinyl Roof Colors and Codes

(A)	Black
(B)	Blue
(D)	Red
(E)	Dove Gray
(H)	Rose
(N)	Lipstick Red
(P)	Silver
(R)	Jade
(T)	Brown
(U)	Chamois
(V)	Creme
(W)	White

Town Landau Model Special Features
Bumper guards front and rear
Front cornering lamps
Wide color-keyed bodyside moldings

Dual sport mirrors
Die-cast Thunderbird hood ornament
Pinstripes on bodyside, hood, grille opening
   panel, decklid, headlamp, doors
Accent paint on fender louvers
Town Landau script on opera windows
Brushed-aluminum wraparound bar appliqué
Turbine-style cast-aluminum wheels
18oz cut pile luxury carpeting
Quartz crystal day/date clock
Door and quarter panels trimmed in velour with
   wood-tone appliqués and carpet on lower door area
Illuminated vanity visor mirror
High-gloss woodtone appliqués on instrument panel
Courtesy interior lighting
Automatic seat back releases
Color-keyed deluxe seat belts
Split-bench front seat with fold-down center armrest
AM/FM stereo search radio
Luxury two-spoke steering wheel
SelectAire air conditioner with manual temperature
   controls
Automatic parking brake release
Electric door locks
Electric remote trunk lid release
400ci V-8
Power Lock Group
Power windows
Special sound insulation
Tilt-Away steering wheel
Tinted glass
Steel-belted WSW radial tires
Trip odometer
Intermittent windshield wipers

Prices (February 7, 1977)

Thunderbird two-door hardtop	$5,063
Thunderbird Town Landau	$7,990

Standard engine: 302ci 2-barrel V-8
(California and high-altitude states: 351ci 2-barrel V-8)

Options

351ci 2-barrel V-8	$92
400ci 2-barrel V-8 (standard on Town Landau)	
Two-door hardtop models	$208
SelectAire air conditioner (manual temperature controls; (standard on Town Landau)	
SelectAire air conditioner (automatic temperature controls)	$512
Town Landau	$41
SelectAire air conditioner (automatic	$512
Heavy-duty 90amp alternator	$45
Optional axle ratio 3:1	$14
Traction-Lok differential	$54
Heavy-duty battery 77amp	$17
Color-keyed deluxe seat belts (standard on Town Landau)	$18
Deluxe Bumper Group (standard on Town Landau)	$20
Day/date clock (standard on Town Landau)	$20
Convenience Group (standard on Town Landau)	$96
Cornering lamps (standard on Town Landau)	$43
Exterior decor package	$317-$368
Interior decor package	$299
Electric rear window defroster	$87
California emission system	$70
High-altitude emission system	$22
Tinted glass (standard on Town Landau)	$61
Engine block immersion heater	$20
Illuminated entry system	$51
Sports Instrumentation Group	$103-$111
Light Group (standard on Town Landau)	$46
Power Lock Group (standard on Town Landau)	$92
Luggage compartment trim (standard on Town Landau)	$38
Luxury Interior Group (standard on Town Landau)	$724
Dual sport mirrors (standard on Town Landau)	$51
Outside chrome-plated left-hand remote mirror	$14
Illuminated visor vanity mirror (standard on Town Landau)	$46
Rocker panel moldings (standard on Town Landau)	$28
Vinyl insert body molding	$39
Wide bright body molding	$39
Wide color-keyed insert body molding	$51
Power moonroof	$888
Metallic Glow paints	$62
Protection Group	$43-$47
AM/FM monaural radio	$59
AM/FM stereo search radio (standard on Town Landau)	$276
AM/FM stereo radio	$120
AM/FM stereo radio with tape player	$193
AM/FM stereo radio with Quadrasonic tape player	$326
Town Landau	
AM/FM stereo radio with Quadrasonic tape player	$50
Two-piece vinyl roof	$132
Six-way full-width power seat	$143
Six-way driver power seat	$143
Bucket seats and console	$158
Automatic seat back release (standard on Town Landau)	$32
Dual rear seat radio speakers	$43
Fingertip speed control	
Town Landau	$93
Hardtop	$114
Sport steering wheel black leather models	
With Sport Instrument Group	$39
Non-Sport Instrument Group	$61
Tilt-Away steering wheel (standard on Town Landau)	$63
Dual accent paint stripes (standard on Town Landau)	$39
Handling suspension	
Town Landau	$34
Hardtop	$79
Space saver spare tire	$13
Trailer-towing package	$138
All-vinyl seat trim (standard on bucket seat option)	$22
Leather and vinyl seat trim (available only on Town Landau or on cars with interior decor package or Luxury Decor Group)	$241
Two-tone paint trim	$49
Wire wheel covers	$99
Turbine-spoke cast-aluminum wheels (standard on Town Landau)	
Models with exterior decor package	$88
All other models	$234
Power side windows (standard on Town Landau)	$114
Five HR78x15 WSW steel-belted radials	$45
Five HR78x15 wide-band WSW steel-belted radials	$61
Five HR70x15 wide-oval steel-belted radials (standard with handling suspension)	$67
Five HR70x15 wide-oval steel-belted radials (Town Landau)	$22

remote trunk lid release, steel-belted radial whitewall tires, an upgraded interior with complimentary trim, and other niceties.

With these lower prices, the Thunderbird was now available to a much wider audience, and the public's response surpassed everyone's projections. By the time the last 1977 model left the assembly lines, Ford had sold about 315,000 Thunderbirds, a phenomenal success story for any car, let alone the Thun-

Another Ghia-influenced Thunderbird design. Note that this car features a different grille than was used on the other exercise.

derbird which in its previous best year sold no better than one-third that amount. In 1977, the Thunderbird was the right car, at the right price, at the right time.

1978

Minor changes were made to the Thunderbird for 1978, mostly updating color and trim selections and adding some Thunderbird emblems to the headlight doors. These were the obvious changes. Other changes that weren't so apparent included a revised, more efficient torque converter; a new, lightweight battery; a revised air induction system for the engine; and a new, lightweight power steering pump with quick disconnect fittings.

There were three Thunderbird models from which to choose: one standard model and two deluxe versions. The standard model, base priced at $5,411, was the Thunderbird two-door hardtop. Moving up a notch was the Town Landau, again at a base price of $8,420. If you wanted a fancier, more exclusive Thunderbird than that, Ford offered a very special model called the Diamond Jubilee Edition at a base price of $10,106. This

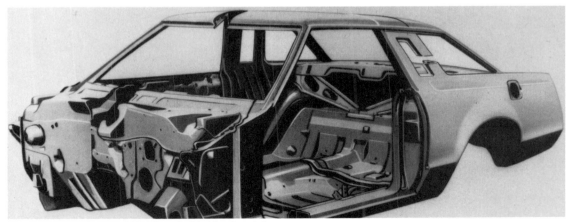

Ever wonder what a 1977 Thunderbird body might look like in the bare metal? *Ford Motor Company*

The new Thunderbirds were good-looking cars even from the rear, as this 1977 promotional photograph shows. *Ford Motor Company*

model was intended as a special commemorative edition to celebrate Ford's 75th anniversary in 1978. Despite their extremely high price tag, Ford sold almost 19,000 Diamond Jubilees.

If you wanted a sporty-looking Thunderbird this year, Ford offered the "sports decor" package, which included a vinyl top with color-keyed backlite moldings; dual accent paint stripes on the hood, bodyside, decklid, and fender louvers; decklid straps; special road wheels with a poly-coated chamois-colored

accent paint; sport mirrors; blackout paint on the vertical bars in the grille; wide bodyside moldings; and HR70x14in white letter tires. This package cost $396–446, depending on other packages ordered.

About midway through the 1978 model year, Ford offered a new option for the Thunderbird meant to appeal to open air devotees who wanted the comfort and safety of a hardtop. This T-Roof Convertible Option was priced at $699, and consisted of two removable glass panels and a black vinyl storage

Without a convertible option available to please open air fans, Ford did the next best thing by offering a T-Top option for the 1978 Thunderbirds. This afforded the security of a hardtop with most of the openness that a convertible offered. *Ford Motor Company*

bag to protect them when they weren't in place.

The 1977 model year had been a banner year as far as sales went, and 1978 was even better, with about 325,000 new Thunderbirds sold. This would be the highest sales figure for any Thunderbird year in its history.

1979

The biggest news for the 1979 model year at Ford Motor Company didn't concern any of its automotive products. Except for the new Mustang and Capri, the new cars were carried over with only minor revisions. No, the biggest news item concerned the firing of Lee Iacocca by Henry Ford II. Like Bunkie Knudsen before him, Iacocca had to go because Henry felt he was starting to get a little too powerful for his own good. Iacocca was fired in October 1978 shortly after the 1979 models were released. He didn't stay unemployed too long, though, for within a month he

signed on to help save a struggling Chrysler Corporation.

The automotive industry wasn't very healthy in the late-1970s, which meant that money to invest in new models had to be carefully spent. Most of the development money available at Ford in the late-1970s was devoted to designing and marketing a new Mustang and Capri; they made their public debuts as new 1979 models in the fall of 1978.

Bowing at the same time were the Thunderbirds, which for 1979 featured a redesigned grille and the switch back to a two-taillight system. Once again, there were three Thunderbird models from which to choose: one standard model and two deluxe versions. The standard, or base model, was the Thunderbird two-door hardtop, and the deluxe versions were the Town Landau and the Thunderbird Heritage, the latter which offered the same equipment and niceties as the Diamond Jubilee and was priced similarly.

In 1979, the Thunderbird showroom catalog carried an aircraft theme, as this cover photograph shows. Also note the "Come Fly With Me" slogan.

During 1979, the Arabs again cut off our oil supply, a further blow to a U.S. economy that was already in a recession. It was a year full of bad economic news, but still the Thunderbird sold fairly well, with numbers above the 280,000 mark. In the course of three model years, 1977–1979, almost one million Thunderbirds were produced—which means there are many Thunderbirds available for collectors fond of this era. For those looking for limited editions to restore, there are the Diamond Jubilee Editions or the Heritage models. The Town Landaus offer luxury touches if you are so inclined, and don't forget the Sports Appearance or T-Top Convertible Packages if you like your Thunderbirds sporty.

1979

Exterior Colors and Codes
(1C)   Black
(1G)   Silver Metallic
(1N)   Dove Gray
(2J)   Maroon (Heritage only)
(2M)   Dark Red
(3F)   Light Medium Blue
(3L)   Midnight Blue Metallic
(46)   Dark Jade Metallic
(5P)   Pastel Chamois
(8N)   Dark Cordovan Metallic
(83)   Light Chamois
(9D)   Polar White
(2H)   Red Glow
(3H)   Medium Blue Glow
(5N)   Burnt Orange Glow
(7L)   Light Jade Glow
(8W)   Chamois Glow

Heritage Thunderbird Features
Special top with filled-in quarter windows and a thick vinyl roof pad
Leather-wrapped steering wheel
Power antenna
Rocker panel moldings
Door plaques with owner's initials
Split-bench front seat with unique seat cover in soft cloth with Thunderbird emblems on seat backs
Assist straps on front seat back and on door panels
36oz luxury carpeting
Molded door and quarter panel armrests with extra padding
Hand-stitched leather-covered pad on instrument panel
Ebony wood-tone appliqués on instrument panel, knobs, door and quarter panels, and steering wheel center
Sports Instrumentation Group

Illuminated visor vanity mirrors
Bright pedal trim pieces
Color-keyed 18oz trunk carpeting
Molded decklid liner
Fingertip speed control
Convenience Group
Light Group
Illuminated entry system
Heritage emblems
Choice of Maroon (2J) or Light Medium Blue (3F) colors
Color-keyed grille, bumper guards, rub strips, cast-aluminum turbine wheels, and triple-band body tape stripes

Town Landau Features
Cast-aluminum wheels with accent paint
Accent pinstripes on hood, body, grille opening panel, decklid, headlamp doors, and fender louvers
15in steel-belted WSW radial tires
Dual remote control sports mirrors
Wide color-coordinated body moldings
Front cornering lamps
Bumper rub strips
Extended-range fuel tank (26gal)

Sports Decor Group Features
Black with Chamois interior
Polar White with Chamois or white interior
Midnight Blue with Chamois interior
Dark Cordovan Metallic with Chamois interior
Dark Jade with Chamois or Jade-colored interior
Burnt Orange with Chamois or white interior
Chamois-colored vinyl roof, bodyside moldings,
Chamois-colored cast-aluminum road wheels
Chamois decklid straps and paint striping on hood, grille panel opening, and fender louvers
Color-keyed remote control sports mirrors
Blacked-out vertical grille bars

This is a 1979 Thunderbird promotional photograph released by Ford of Canada in 1978. *Ford of Canada*

A 1978 Thunderbird equipped with Ford's Sports Decor equipment package, which included striping, sport mirrors, chamois-colored polycast wheels, vinyl top, and side moldings. Another interesting feature was the leather straps on the trunk lid. *Ford Motor Company*

The 1979 Thunderbird Town Landau. Note the cast-aluminum, turbine-style wheels and stainless steel roof band. *Ford Motor Company*

Chapter 10

1980-1982: Luxury in a Smaller Package

★★★★★	1980 Thunderbird Silver Anniversary Edition
★★★★	1980 Thunderbird Town Landau
★★★	1980 Thunderbird Two-door
★★★★★	1981 Thunderbird Heritage
★★★	1981 Thunderbird Town Landau
★★★	1981 Thunderbird Two-door
★★★★★	1982 Thunderbird Heritage
★★★★	1982 Thunderbird Town Landau
★★★	1982 Thunderbird Two-door

Back in 1976—when the largest Thunderbirds still roamed the streets—work began on a new Thunderbird to meet the needs of the 1980s. When the 1976 Thunderbird was on the drawing board, hardly any consideration was given to high fuel economy numbers, but such was not the case when work started on the 1980 Thunderbird. Decent fuel economy numbers were of prime importance now thanks to a federally mandated program called Corporate Average Fuel Economy (CAFE), slated to take effect during the 1980 model year. In essence, the federal government mandated that starting in 1980, a U.S. automotive manufacturer's lineup had to average 20mpg—and those fuel economy requirements would get more stringent after

1980. So, Ford's number one priority during the mid- to late-1970s was to build cars that were more fuel-efficient for the 1980s.

For the Thunderbird, that meant going on another crash diet to lose more weight and inches. The downsized 1977–1979 models

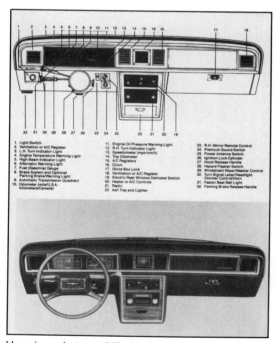

Here is a photo and illustration of the new-for-1980 Thunderbird's dashboard layout. *Ford Motor Company*

A Ford designer works on a clay model before it goes into a wind tunnel. *Ford Motor Company*

The new-for-1980 Thunderbird was shorter and more square than the models it replaced. This photo shows a new Thunderbird Town Landau. *Ford Motor Company*

were more fuel-efficient than the 1976 version, but their figures still weren't high enough to meet the requirements.

1980

Once again, the Thunderbird became a unibody car with front and rear subframes, rather than a full-frame unit. The new unibody package sat on a shortened 108.4in wheelbase (down 5.6in), and its overall length was reduced 16.8in, to 200.4in. The new Thunderbird's width was also thinned down a bit from 78.5in to 74.1in. The resultant Thunderbird weighed 800lb less than its 1979 predecessor.

But reduced weight alone wasn't going to get the Thunderbird the mileage figures it needed to help Ford reach its CAFE goal. Ford was going to have to rely on some help from other areas, one of which was aerodynamics. If the body could be given a more effective wind-cheating shape it would decrease resistance, and increased mileage figures might follow. Clay models of the Thunderbird went through more than 250 hours of wind tunnel testing at the University of Maryland. When that initial testing was complete, some fiberglass models underwent an addi-

Customers wanting a special Thunderbird in 1980 could order a Silver Anniversary Edition, as this ad shows.

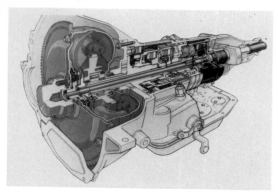

An illustration of Ford's new four-speed Automatic OverDrive (AOD) transmission. *Ford Motor Company*

Look at all that soft leather. Ford really knew how to outfit a Thunderbird interior in the early-1980s. *Ford Motor Company*

tional 150 hours of testing at Lockheed's Low-Speed Wind Tunnel.

The results of all this testing showed the Ford designers where they could improve the Thunderbird so that it would slip through the air with a lower coefficient of drag (CD). The new Thunderbird's final coefficient of drag was 0.44, compared to 0.51 for the 1979 Thunderbird. That was an impressive gain and one that would help the Thunderbird reach its 20mpg goal.

The new Thunderbird may have been smaller on the outside, but the Ford designers and package planners managed to increase the interior room as well as the trunk capacity over previous models. Rear seat legroom was increased by about 4in and trunk capacity grew by approximately 2cu-ft.

A new base engine was fitted to the new Thunderbird, a smaller version of Ford's small-block V-8 that displaced some 255ci or 4.2-liters. This engine used most of the same parts as the 302, but the engine was 60lb lighter and, according to Ford, put out a little more horsepower than the 302. Development work on this engine began in 1977 with the goal being to produce smaller and lighter engines that could generate the same amount of power as the bigger engines they would replace. By following this route, Ford hoped

Here is an example of what a 1981 Thunderbird looked like when painted in a two-tone scheme. *Ford Motor Company*

that the weight saved would help boost fuel economy figures and improve handling. The 302 was still available as an extra cost option.

A new engine wasn't the only powertrain change Ford offered on the 1980 Thunderbirds. For those customers who ordered the 302ci V-8 engine, Ford offered as optional equipment a new transmission known as the AOD transmission, an acronym that stood for Automatic OverDrive. This transmission was a four-speed automatic, with overdrive as the top gear. This extra overdrive gear was claimed to improve fuel economy by 45 percent on the highway and 21 percent in the city. What that boils down to in real figures is an increase of 2–3mpg. Every little bit helped, and that 302/AOD combination probably helped Ford reach the federal 20mpg mileage target.

Only two models were available at the start of the 1980 model year: the Thunderbird and the Thunderbird Town Landau.

Even though the Thunderbird was the base model, it came pretty well equipped, with a 4.2-liter V-8, SelectShift automatic transmission, power front disc brakes, a flight bench seat, a chrome-plated grille, MacPherson strut front suspension, variable ratio power steering, P-metric-sized steel-belted radial tires, concealed rectangular headlamps, inside hood release, trip odometer, and a host of other amenities.

The deluxe version, also known as the Town Landau, came with all the base model's features plus soft velour seat coverings, 18oz luxury carpeting, luxury door and quarter trim panels, wood-tone appliqués, Tilt-Away steering wheel, electronic instrument cluster, diagnostic warning lights, an engraved owner's nameplate, SelectAire air conditioner, power windows and door locks, a padded-rear-half vinyl top, opera windows, an electronic AM/FM stereo search radio, and an AutoLamp Off-On-Delay headlight system.

If one wanted a more exclusive model than the Town Landau, Ford offered a special Thunderbird model starting on January 1, 1980. This special model was called the Silver Anniversary Thunderbird in honor of the model's twenty-fifth anniversary. These cars featured a special silver metallic finish called Anniversary Silver Glow and a special silver-colored vinyl top with a black wraparound band. They also featured special black pinstriping, black accents around the windows, air conditioning, power windows, power disc brakes, speed control, a digital speedometer, a keyless entry system, a special owner's nameplate, AOD transmission, and other goodies.

As if there wasn't enough newness to please buyers in 1980, Ford offered some ad-

---

1980
Silver Anniversary Thunderbird Features

Special silver exterior paint
Gray velour interior
AM/FM stereo search radio
SelectAire air conditioner
Power windows and seats
Power brakes
Power antenna
Speed control
Whitewall radial tires
Special owner's nameplate
Digital speedometer
Keyless entry system
Automatic overdrive transmission
Black wraparound roof band
Black strips on front fascia, rear fascia, and
    body moldings
Black pinstriping
Black accents around windows
Black coated exterior mirrors

Exterior Colors and Codes

(8D)	Bittersweet Glow
(8W)	Chamois Glow
(9D)	Polar White
(2H)	Red Glow
(1G)	Silver Metallic
(1C)	Black
(12)	Light Gray
(8N)	Dark Cordovan Metallic
(6D)	Pastel Sand
(8A)	Dark Chamois Metallic
(3H)	Medium Blue Glow
(7M)	Dark Pine Metallic
(3L)	Midnight Blue Metallic
(2K)	Candyapple Red

Two-tone Color Choices

Polar White over Bittersweet Glow
Polar White over Midnight Blue Metallic
Silver Metallic over Black
Black over Silver Metallic
Silver Metallic over Dark Cordovan Metallic
Midnight Blue Metallic over Medium Blue Glow
Chamois Glow over Dark Chamois Metallic
Bittersweet Glow over Dark Cordovan Metallic

In 1981, this Heritage model replaced the Silver Anniversary Edition of 1980 as the top-of-the-line model. *Ford Motor Company*

ditional options to make the Thunderbird even more special. One of these new features was called a keyless entry system, whereby the owner could unlock the car by punching in a series of numbers from a dialing pad in the upper door. Another special feature was the electronic digital dashboard, an option that really added a high-tech look to the Thunderbird's instrument panel. A third option worthy of note was the TRX wheel and tire combination which greatly improved the Thunderbird's handling prowess. No matter how you look at it, 1980 was a great year to buy a Thunderbird because of all the neat improvements Ford made to the car.

1981

Although it had to put in some extra effort to do so, Ford Motor Company improved the Thunderbird for model year 1981.

Once again, there were three models from which to choose: the Thunderbird, Thunderbird Town Landau, and making a return engagement, the Thunderbird Heritage.

If there was any doubt that fuel economy was a top priority for the Thunderbird it was put aside when Ford announced that the base Thunderbird engine for 1981 would be the 3.3-liter I-Block inline six-cylinder, otherwise known as the 200ci six—the same engine that powered Ford's 1970s era Maverick economy

This Town Landau coupe was the mid-range model in the 1981 Thunderbird lineup. It still looked pretty chic, even though it was not the top-of-the-line model. *Ford Motor Company*

1981

Heritage Standard Equipment Features

Padded-rear-half vinyl roof with wraparound band in brushed-aluminum
Coach lamps
Frenched backlight
Decklid striping
Front cornering lamps
Rocker panel moldings
Wire wheel covers
Electronic instrument cluster
Six-way power driver seat
Illuminated visor vanity mirror
Electronic digital clock
Power windows
Power door locks
AutoLamp Off-On-Delay headlight system
AM/FM stereo search radio
Tinted glass
Air conditioning
Bright rhodium-engraved personalized nameplate on instrument panel
Crushed-velour seat coverings
Luxury steering wheel
Luxury door and quarter panel trim
Automatic parking brake release
Burled rosewood woodtone accents
Courtesy lamps
Luxury luggage compartment trim
Unique hood ornament with cut-glass inserts
Heritage fender scripts

Town Landau Standard Equipment Features

Padded rear half-vinyl roof
Color-coordinated roof wraparound band
Coach lamps
Dual remote control exterior mirrors
Striping on hood and bodysides
Luxury wheel covers
Split-bench front seat
Knit cloth upholstery
Tilt-Away steering wheel
Diagnostic warning lights
AM/FM stereo
Intermittent windshield wipers
Decorated door panels with assist straps
Armrest pads on quarter panel trim
Wood-tone instrument panel appliqué
Wide door and bodyside moldings

Exterior Colors and Codes

(1C)	Black
(1G)	Silver Metallic
(1P)	Medium Gray Metallic
(3F)	Light Medium Blue
(3L)	Midnight Blue Metallic
(8N)	Dark Cordovan Metallic
(9D)	Polar White
(12)	Light Gray
(24)	Red
(89)	Fawn
(3H)	Medium Blue Glow
(5H)	Light Fawn Glow
(8D)	Bittersweet Glow
(55)	Medium Fawn Glow

Two-tone Combinations

Upper Color: Midnight Blue Metallic
Lower Color: Medium Blue Glow
Upper Color: Red
Lower Color: Fawn
Upper Color: Fawn
Lower Color: Medium Fawn Glow
Upper Color: Black
Lower Color: Silver Metallic
Upper Color: Bittersweet Glow
Lower Color: Dark Cordovan Metallic

sedan. For the first time in Thunderbird history, a V-8 engine wasn't standard fare. As extra-cost options, the Thunderbird buyer could choose either the 255ci engine, or Ford's 302, both of which were available with the optional four-speed AOD transmission. Six-cylinder buyers had to be satisfied with the three-speed SelectShift automatic transmission. The new 200ci six-cylinder engine was not the only change for the 1981 models. They differed from their 1980 counterparts in that they came with halogen headlights, and the lower grille piece found on the 1980 model's front fascia was now gone. Otherwise, the cars looked basically the same. Under the hood a viscous clutch was added to the fans of all 1981 Thunderbird engines to reduce parasitic horsepower losses. And for those who still craved the look of a convertible top, one of Ford's new-for-1981 options was a simulated convertible top—the dashing look of a sporty convertible without the hassle of cold drafts, leaking rain, or somebody slicing up the top to gain access to the interior.

1982

For 1982, the Thunderbird buyer had a choice of two six-cylinder engines and one V-8. Once again, the inline 200ci six-cylinder was the base engine for the Thunderbird. The oth-

1982

Options

(prices given are for the options if purchased separately)

Premium sound system:	
Conventional stereo radio	$133
Electronic stereo radio	$167
Flip-open air roof	$276
Carriage roof:	
With exterior decor option cars	$766
All Others	$973
Rear-half vinyl roof	$156
Luxury rear-half vinyl roof:	
With exterior decor package	$163
Thunderbird	$320
Bucket seats and console (standard on Town Landau and Luxury Decor) No charge	
All others	$211
Recaro bucket seats:	
Heritage	$222
Interior luxury option	$405
Town Landau and Thunderbird	$523
Split-bench seat	$206
All-vinyl seat trim	$28
Super Soft vinyl split-bench seat trim	$30
Ultra Soft leather split-bench trim	$409
Six-way power seat, split-bench (standard on Heritage)	$198
Fingertip speed control	$155
Leather-wrapped luxury steering wheel	$51
Tilt-Away steering wheel (standard on Heritage or Town Landau)	$95
Dual accent bodyside paint stripes (standard on Heritage, Town Landau, or Luxury Decor package)	$49
Hood and bodyside accent paint striping	$65
Exterior Decor package striping	$16
Heavy-duty suspension system	$26
Tripminder computer:	
Heritage, Luxury Group, or Electronic Instrumentation Cluster	$215
All others	$261
Pivoting front vent windows	$63
Luxury wheel covers (standard on Town Landau or Exterior Decor package)	$107
Wire wheel covers (standard on Heritage)	
Town Landau or Exterior Decor package	$45
Thunderbird hardtop	$152
Power side windows (standard on Heritage or Interior Luxury Group)	$165
Interval windshield wipers (standard on Heritage, Town Landau, or Interior Luxury Group)	$48
California emission control system	$65
High-altitude emission system	No Charge
3.8ltr 232ci six (standard on Heritage)	$241
4.2ltr 255ci V-8 (standard on Heritage)	$241
Traction-Lok rear axle	$76
SelectAire air conditioner automatic temperature controls	
Heritage	$78

All Others	$754
SelectAire air conditioner manual temperature controls (standard for Heritage)	$676
AutoLamp Off-On-Delay headlight system (standard on Heritage)	$73
Heavy-duty battery	$24
Lower-body protection	
Heritage	$39
All others	$54
Electronic digital clock (standard on Heritage)	$46
Front cornering lamps (standard on Heritage)	$59
Electric rear window defroster	$126
Diagnostic warning lights (standard on Heritage, Town Landau, and Luxury Decor Interior Group)	$59
Exterior Decor package (Not available on Heritage or Town Landau)	$385
Tinted glass (Standard on Heritage)	88
Immersion engine block heater	$17
Illuminated entry system (standard on cars with keyless entry)	$68
Electronic instrument cluster (standard/$321 credit on Heritage)	
Interior Luxury Group	$321
Thunderbird	$367
Interior Decor package (standard on Town Landau)	$372
Interior Luxury package (standard on Heritage)	
Town Landau	$683
All others	$1,204
Keyless entry system	$139
Light Group (standard on Heritage, Town Landau, or Luxury Decor Interior package)	$35
Power Lock Group (standard on Heritage)	$138
Luxury compartment trim	$48
Dual illuminated visor vanity mirrors	
Heritage or Luxury Interior package	$46
All others	$91
Right-hand remote control mirror (standard on Heritage, Town Landau, or Exterior Decor package)	$60
Wide door belt moldings (standard on Heritage, Town Landau, or Exterior Decor package)	$51
Metallic Glow paint	$80
Two-tone paint	
Heritage	$128
Town Landau	$141
Exterior Decor package	$157
Two-door hardtop	$206
Automatic parking brake release (standard on Heritage or Luxury Decor Interior package)	$12
Appearance Protection Group	$51
AM radio rear seat speakers	$39
AM/FM monaural radio	$54
AM/FM monaural radio rear seat speakers	$39
AM/FM stereo radio (standard on Town Landau)	$85
AM/FM stereo with eight-track tape player	
Town Landau	$87
Two-door hardtop	$172
AM/FM stereo with cassette tape player	
Town Landau	$87

Two-door hardtop	$172	Heritage		$87
Electronic Search AM/FM stereo radio		Town Landau		$233
(standard on Heritage)		Two-door hardtop		$318
Town Landau	$146	Power radio antenna		$55
Two-door hardtop	$232	AM radio Delete Option Credit		$61
Electronic AM/FM Stereo Search radio with		P195/75R14 Puncture-resistant self-sealing		
eight-track tape player		WSW		$106
Heritage	$87	TR-Type radial tires with special TRX wheels		
Town Landau	$233	Heritage		$490
Two-door hardtop	$318	Town Landau or Exterior Decor package		$535
Electronic AM/FM stereo search radio with		Two-door hardtop		$643
cassette tape player and Dolby Noise		Conventional spare tire		$51
Reduction System				

The last of the small, squared-off Thunderbird coupes. In 1983, the Thunderbird would take on a new, more rounded, aerodynamic look. *Ford Motor Company*

er six was a new 3.8-liter (232ci) V-6, an engine that posted a very decent 30mpg on the highway and 18mpg in the city. Ford didn't publish horsepower figures for its engines in 1982, so we can't say with certainty which engine was more powerful, but people who have driven cars equipped with both engines say the V-6 feels more powerful than the in-line six. In addition to these six-cylinder engines, the 255ci V-8 was still available as an option. Ford's AOD four-speed automatic transmission was available for both the 3.8-liter V-6 and the 255ci V-8, and a much improved, more efficient, three-speed SelectShift transmission was offered as standard equipment on both six-cylinder engines.

To boost the driving range, a larger, 21gal gasoline tank replaced the former 18gal version. As an added fuel economy booster, Ford offered a new, onboard computer called the Tripminder which continuously monitored fuel flow, speed, and real or elapsed time to destination.

Other changes to the 1982 Thunderbird included two new vinyl roof treatments, upgraded interior components, and exterior trim updates.

All in all, 1982 was a pretty good year to spread your wings behind the wheel of a new Thunderbird.

Chapter 11

1983-1986: The Aero Look Comes on Strong

★★★	1983 Thunderbird
★★★★	1983 Thunderbird Heritage
★★★★	1983 Thunderbird Turbo Coupe
★★★	1984 Thunderbird
★★★★	1984 Thunderbird élan
★★★★	1984 Thunderbird FILA
★★★★	1984 Thunderbird Turbo Coupe
★★★	1985 Thunderbird
★★★★	1985 Thunderbird élan
★★★★	1985 Thunderbird FILA
★★★★	1985 Thunderbird Turbo Coupe
★★★★★	1985 Thunderbird 30th Anniversary Edition
★★★	1986 Thunderbird
★★★★	1986 Thunderbird élan
★★★★	1986 Thunderbird Turbo Coupe

Ever since the first ones hit the streets back in the mid-1950s, Thunderbirds have been trendsetters. If you have any doubts about that claim, all you have to do is think about porthole tops, bucket seats and consoles, swing-away steering columns, and vinyl tops, which were all introduced and made popular by the Thunderbird.

Thunderbirds have always been leaders in the automotive world, as was again proven in the fall of 1982, when a new, aerodynamically designed Thunderbird burst on the scene. And burst it did, with a radical new look that was daringly different from the square, subdued look of the previous Thunderbirds.

1983

A top priority during the early stages of the new Thunderbird's development was to design a car that could attain reasonable fuel economy numbers. The product planners, designers, stylists, and engineers had already lightened the Thunderbird as much as possible, so they decided to concentrate on making the new Thunderbird a little more slippery.

Once again during its development stages, the Thunderbird would spend more than 500 hours in a wind tunnel perfecting air

This promotional postcard shows the new-for-1983 Thunderbird Turbo Coupe. *Ford Motor Company*

Another 1983 Thunderbird promotional postcard, showing a regular model. *Ford Motor Company*

flow management. When the testing was over, the Thunderbird team had a car with a slippery shape and a coefficient of drag of 0.35, a rating that beat the old mark of 0.44 by a substantial margin. The end result was a car that was stylish, aerodynamically clean, and miles ahead of the domestic mid-size competition—the Buick Regal, Oldsmobile Cutlass Supreme, Chevrolet Monte Carlo, Pontiac Grand Prix, Chrysler Cordoba, and Dodge Mirada. The Thunderbird was the leader of the pack again.

Comparisons

1980–1982 Thunderbirds	1983–1986 Thunderbirds
Wheelbase: 108.4in	Wheelbase: 104in
Length: 200.4in	Length: 197.6in
Height: 53in	Height: 53.2in
Width: 74.4in	Width: 71.1in
Tread front: 58.1in	Tread front: 58.1in
Tread rear: 57in	Tread rear: 58.5in
Curb weight: 3,350lb	Curb weight: Base 3,089lb Turbo Coupe 3,172lb

The new Thunderbirds caused quite a sensation when they were introduced in the fall of 1982, appearing on the covers of several national magazines, which helped to draw potential customers to Ford's showrooms. These cars were image boosters for Ford in that they showed that the company was committed to the very latest in design trends and technology, attributes that appealed to a younger, more sophisticated market than the Thunderbird had attracted previously. As a matter of fact, some of the traditional clientele balked at the Thunderbird's new aerodynamic look. Surveys confirmed that buyers forty years old and over generally preferred the earlier Thunderbird look, whereas buyers in the under-forty age group overwhelmingly preferred the new look. This news bode well for the future of Thunderbird sales and told Ford it had selected the right route.

Initially, there were only two Thunderbird models and one engine from which to choose: the base Thunderbird and an upscale deluxe version called the Heritage. In base form, the new Thunderbird offered such niceties as reclining front bucket seats and a console, power rack and pinion steering, gas-

The FILA was a special Thunderbird model that Ford first offered in 1984. Perfect for the label-conscious, mid-1980s consumer, FILAs featured special paint, trim, and accessories.

This 1985 Thunderbird features a rather unique powerplant. When was the last time you saw a 427 SOHC engine in a car this modern?

filled shocks, a 3.8-liter V-6 engine and three-speed automatic transmission, and electronic ignition.

In addition to the standard items found in the base Thunderbird, the Heritage came equipped with an electronic instrument cluster with a digital speedometer display and several LEDs (light-emitting diodes) in place of the usual gauges and dials found on other cars, a digital electronic clock, diagnostic warning light display, automatic Off-On-Delay headlight system, dual illuminated visor mirrors, wood-tone interior appliqués, power windows, 16oz luxury carpeting, and coach lamps mounted to the roof C panels.

On February 1, 1983, Ford introduced a new Thunderbird model called the Turbo Coupe, the first Thunderbird ever with a four-cylinder engine. The Turbo Coupe's engine was no ordinary four-cylinder engine by any means, however, as a Garrett AIResearch T-03 turbocharger boosted its output to 145hp at 4600rpm. That was a rating of more than 1hp per cubic inch displacement because the 2.3-liter engine displaced 130ci.

This new Turbo Coupe was aimed at the driver who wanted a Thunderbird with sporting characteristics rather than one with a luxurious touch. In addition to the turbocharged engine exclusive to this model, it came equipped with a five-speed manual/overdrive transmission and a Traction-Lok rear end. This five-speed transmission was the only one offered on the Turbo Coupe and the

---

1983

Turbo Coupe
2.3-liter OHC four-cylinder turbocharged engine
Five-speed/manual/overdrive transmission
Power front disc brakes
Power rack and pinion steering
Modified MacPherson Strut front suspension
Gas-filled shocks
Tachometer
Boost/overboost lights
Special handling package
Quad rear shocks
Traction-Lok rear axle 3.45:1 ratio
P205/70HR14 Goodyear performance radials
DuraSpark electronic ignition
Windshield washers
Quad halogen headlamps
Dual electric remote exterior mirrors
Special charcoal or black accents
Wide body moldings
Unique front fascia with airdam
Marchal fog lamps
Body and decklid stripes
Unique 14in aluminum wheels
Articulated front bucket seats
Fishnet map pockets on door panels
Tunnel-mounted floor shifter with leather-wrapped knob
16oz luxury carpet
Electronic digital clock
AM/FM stereo radio
Leather-wrapped sports steering wheel
Luxury trunk compartment trim
Diagnostic warning lights
Light Group

Turbo Coupe Exterior Colors
Black
Pastel Charcoal
Bright Red
Light Desert Tan
Silver
Dark Charcoal
Medium Red

Turbo Coupe Interior Choices
Charcoal
Medium Red
Desert Tan
Paint Stripes: Medium Gray, Maroon, Dark Tan

Thunderbird Exterior Colors
Black
Polar White
Pastel Charcoal
Red
Light Academy Blue
Pastel Vanilla
Desert Tan
Dark Charcoal
Silver*
Medium Red*
Midnight Academy Blue*
Walnut*
*Optional Clearcoat Metallic Colors

Thunderbird Interior Colors
Charcoal
Medium Red
Academy Blue
Walnut
Desert Tan
Opal with Charcoal
Opal with Red
Opal with Blue
Opal with Tan

lack of an automatic transmission might have limited its appeal, but this small detriment was more than offset by the performance boost (pardon the pun) that this car gave to the Thunderbird line. Some went so far as to say this Turbo Coupe Thunderbird was as good, and better in some cases, than some European or Japanese sport coupes, and even bolder individuals claimed that the Turbo Coupe was an "Americanized BMW," quite a compliment considering BMW's lofty perch at that time. The Turbo Coupe's primary competition in 1983 came from the Buick Regal Turbo, Datsun 280ZX, Audi 5000 Turbo, Toyota Celica Supra, Volvo Turbo, Saab 900 Turbo, and BMW 320i and 633csi—impressive company.

At the same time that it released the Turbo Coupe, Ford added the 5.0-liter 302ci V-8 to the Thunderbird's option list. Now, if buyers wanted a little more power than the base 3.8-liter V-6 provided, they could once again order a V-8-powered Thunderbird.

With all this radical change, how did the new Thunderbird fare against the old? During 1982, 45,142 Thunderbirds were produced, whereas in 1983, 122,000 new Thunderbirds left the assembly lines. That's an increase of better than 76,000 units. The Thunderbird hadn't topped the 100,000 unit mark since 1980. This record-breaker was a good indication that the Thunderbird was once again on the right track.

1984

After spending millions of dollars developing and tooling up for the new 1983 Thunderbird, little money remained available to make any radical changes for 1984. Consequently, the changes that were made, though minor in scope, were designed to make the Thunderbird more appealing.

One thing Ford did was expand the Thunderbird line to four distinct models. Once again, the base model was called Thunderbird. Next on the agenda were two deluxe versions called the Thunderbird élan and the Thunderbird FILA. Rounding out the line-up was the high-performance Thunderbird Turbo Coupe.

The Thunderbird élan replaced the Heritage model of the year before. Like the Her-

In 1985, the Thunderbird Turbo Coupe featured a rather involved dashboard, as this promotional photograph shows. *Ford Motor Company*

itage, it came equipped with an electronic instrument cluster, AutoLamp Off-On-Delay headlight system, power windows, power locks, a deluxe interior, and an AM/FM stereo search radio.

The FILA Thunderbird was inspired by FILA sportswear popular with "yuppies" in the mid-1980s. By offering such a model, Ford was probably trying to attract some of those young, label-conscious, upwardly mobile consumers. The FILA Thunderbird came equipped with a 3.8-liter V-6 EFI (electronic fuel injection) engine mated to Ford's AOD four-speed automatic transmission, front cornering lamps, an electronic AM/FM stereo search radio and premium sound system, fingertip speed control, Tilt-Away steering wheel, six-way power driver seat, and more. From the Turbo Coupe it borrowed a special handling package, articulated seats, P205/70HR14 performance tires on color-keyed aluminum road wheels, and a leather-wrapped sports steering wheel. Its exterior was painted Charcoal Pastel over a Dark Charcoal Lower

1984

FILA model
3.8-liter EFI V-6 engine
AOD four-speed automatic overdrive transmission
Variable-ratio power steering
Special handling package
P205/70HR14 black sidewall performance radial tires
Dual electric remote exterior mirrors
Wide body moldings
Front cornering lamps
Color-keyed aluminum road wheels
Articulated front seats
Padded console
Luxury carpeting
Quarter panel trim lights
Leather-wrapped sports steering wheel
Trip odometer
Electric digital clock
Glovebox and ashtray lights
Color-keyed cloth headliner
Inertia seat back releases
Color-keyed deluxe seat belts
Electronic AM/FM stereo search radio with cassette player and Dolby Noise Reduction System
Premium sound system
Power locks
Power windows
Intermittent wipers
Six-way power driver seat
Tinted glass
Tilt-Away steering wheel
Fingertip speed control
AutoLamp Off-On-Delay headlight system
Illuminated entry system
Diagnostic warning lights
Automatic parking brake release
Special Pastel Charcoal/Dark Charcoal two-tone paint
Red/Blue pinstriping
FILA badges

Turbo Coupe
2.3-liter OHC turbocharged four-cylinder engine
Five-speed manual/overdrive transmission
Special handling package
Tachometer
Boost/overboost lights
Traction-Lok rear axle
P205x70HR14 black sidewall Goodyear high-performance tires
14in aluminum wheels
Unique front fascia with air dam and Marchal driving lamps
Wide body moldings
Articulated front seats
Body and decklid striping
Padded console
Luxury carpeting
All-vinyl door panels with assist straps and storage bins
Trip odometer
Electronic digital clock
Color-keyed cloth headliner and sun visors
Utility strap on driver sun visor
Illuminated vanity mirror on passenger sun visor
Inertia seat back releases
AM/FM stereo search radio
Diagnostic warning lights

Exterior Colors
Black
Bright Canyon Red
Midnight Canyon Red
Light Wheat
Wheat
Oxford White
Silver Metallic
Pastel Charcoal/Dark Charcoal (FILA Only)
Dark Charcoal Metallic*
Medium Red Metallic*
Pastel Academy Blue Metallic*
Midnight Academy Blue Metallic*
Light Desert Tan Metallic*
Walnut Metallic*
* Optional Clearcoat Paints

The best of the old and new. This promotional photograph was taken by Ford's Design Center in 1985. In the foreground is a new 30th Anniversary Edition, while a classic 1955 sits in the background. *Ford Motor Company*

The 1985 Thunderbird Turbo Coupe was a pretty slick-looking automobile, as this promotional photograph shows. *Ford Motor Company*

Body Accent Treatment. This combination for 1984 was a FILA Thunderbird exclusive. Special red and blue bodyside and decklid striping complemented its special FILA badges. If you wanted a Thunderbird that would impress your friends or business associates the FILA was the perfect choice.

As in 1983, the Turbo Coupe was again the Thunderbird high-performance offer-ing. The Turbo Coupe came equipped with a high-performance turbocharged engine, a five-speed manual transmission, quad rear shocks, performance-rated, high-speed tires, and a host of other sporty equipment. If you were a driver who liked to drive a Thunderbird to its limits the Turbo Coupe was definitely the way to go.

Although Ford didn't change much for 1984, it was enough to increase the Thunderbird's appeal and generate higher sales and production figures.

1985

The model lineup for the Thunderbird was not changed for 1985, but Ford made several improvements to further increase the Thunderbird's appeal. Most of these were made on the inside, where a redesigned instrument panel featured a new electronic LCD speedometer and gauges. The split-bench front seat and center console were also redesigned, and the rear seat featured a redesigned center fold-down armrest. The articulated seats found in the élan, FILA, and Turbo Coupe cars now featured a power lumbar support system rather than the old manual/squeeze-bulb system used previously.

On the exterior, the 1985 Thunderbird models featured a redesigned grille, a new taillight design, and a redesigned Thunderbird insignia. Tires on the base car were up-

---

1985
30th Anniversary Edition

Special 30th Anniversary Edition badges on instrument panel and decklid
Ignition keys with embossed profiles of 1955 and 1985 models
Floor mats with 30th Anniversary Edition logos
An Owner's Manual folder containing a "Thunderbird History" booklet
Leather jacket with a Thunderbird insignia designed by Member's Only Clothing
5.0-liter V-8
Automatic overdrive four-speed transmission
P225/60VR15 black sidewall "Gatorback" performance radials
15x7in cast-aluminum wheels
Handling suspension
Electronic instrument cluster
Electronic AM/FM stereo search radio with cassette tape player
Graphic equalizer
Electronic climate control system
Speed control
Leather-wrapped Tilt-Away steering wheel
Rear window defroster
Power antenna
Driver and passenger six-way power adjustable seats
Regatta Blue cloth trim
Body color grille, headlight doors, mirrors
Black greenhouse and B-pillar moldings, taillamp appliqués, door handles, door and decklid lock housings
Dark Charcoal radio antenna base

Even though the standard model Thunderbird didn't have as much to offer as the élan, LX, or Turbo Coupe, it was a rather nice-looking car in 1986. *Ford Motor Company*

graded also, from P195/75R14 to P205/70R14. A counterbalanced hood replaced the old prop rod used on earlier cars, and an improved sheet metal corrosion protection process helped keep rust problems at bay. For those buyers who wanted a Turbo Coupe but didn't want to bother with clutching and shifting, a new automatic transmission was offered as an option.

On January 1, 1985, Ford began offering a special limited-edition Thunderbird based on the élan, and called the 30th Anniversary Edition Thunderbird. This limited-production vehicle debuted as a 1985-1/2 model, and Ford is said to have produced about 5,000. These cars were easy to spot, thanks to their special Medium Regatta Blue Clearcoat Metallic color.

1986

For 1986, the Thunderbird lineup contained only three models: the base Thunderbird, Thunderbird élan, and Thunderbird Turbo Coupe. The FILA model was dropped.

A new sequential multi-port fuel injection system was included on the 302ci V-8, and tires on the base Thunderbird and élan were upgraded from the P205/70R14 size used in 1985 to a new P215/70R14 size. A new, high-mounted brake light added a little extra measure of safety and helped reduce the likelihood of rear-end collisions. And the base AM/FM stereo radio was upgraded to include electronic tuning.

Base prices for the 1986 models ranged from $11,020 to $14,143, and a long option list made it easy to raise the price above the base level.

In 1986, 163,965 Thunderbirds rolled off the assembly line, which wasn't too bad for a car whose design was basically unchanged through four model years. A revamped body was one of the changes Thunderbird buyers would see once the 1987 cars made their debut.

A 1986 Turbo Coupe. *Ford Motor Company*

Chapter 12

★★★	1987-1988 Thunderbird
★★★★	1987-1988 Thunderbird LX
★★★★	1987-1988 Thunderbird Sport
★★★★★	1987-1988 Thunderbird Turbo Coupe

1987-1988: Pushing the Aerodynamic Envelope

1987

For 1987, the Thunderbird featured a revamped and restyled body with a more aerodynamic front end and flush-mounted headlights, a new grille, and a new front fascia.

A new roof design with a redesigned rear window and flush-mounted glass flowed smoothly into a raised and redesigned rear decklid. The higher rear deck and new roof, along with the flush glass areas helped air flow more smoothly over the body—in effect, helping the Thunderbird cut through the air easier.

Rounding out the body modifications was a redesigned taillight and rear fascia, new body side moldings, new wheels, and a twin-scooped hood for the Turbo Coupe.

Other changes included a refined front suspension system to help the Thunderbird ride and handle better, some interior updates, and more power for the Turbo Coupe.

In addition to the base Thunderbird and Turbo Coupe, Ford added a new model to the lineup and renamed one of its previous models. The new model was the Thunderbird Sport, and the renamed model was the Thunderbird LX, formerly known as the élan.

The standard model Thunderbird came equipped with a 3.8-liter EFI V-6 engine, Automatic Overdrive four-speed transmission, P215/70R14 all-season radial tires, cloth-covered reclining split-bench seat, air conditioning, and electronic digital instrumentation. It was a lot of car for its base price of $13,460.

This promotional license plate tells it all. In 1987, the Thunderbird Turbo Coupe was selected the *Motor Trend* "Car of the Year."

The 1987 Thunderbird Turbo Coupe featured quite a few changes that make it easy to distinguish from the 1986 model it replaced. There is a new, dual scooped hood, a new header panel, and a new front fascia. *Ford Motor Company*

121

The 1987 Turbo Coupe was a high-performance driver's car, so posing one on a twisty mountain road was only natural. *Ford Motor Company*

The Thunderbird Sport was just the ticket for the sporty buyer. It was equipped with the 5.0-liter V-8 and AOD four-speed transmission as standard equipment. The Sport also came with a handling suspension package, quad rear shocks, and P215/HR70R14 black sidewall speed-rated performance tires. Other niceties included black exterior accents, styled road wheels, Traction-Lok rear axle, dual-note sports horns, bucket seats with console and floor shifter, Special Light Group, and a leather-wrapped sports steering wheel. The Thunderbird Sport was available for a base price of $15,497.

If luxury was your desire the luxurious Thunderbird LX was the car of choice. Standard features included speed control, power windows, dual electric remote control mirrors, an electronic digital clock, intermittent wipers, diagnostic warning lights, a Tilt-Away steering wheel, automatic parking brake release on V-6 models, an electronic AM/FM radio with cassette tape player, an illuminated entry system, power locks, power driver's seat, accent striping on the body sides and decklid, LX emblems, styled road wheels, and a leather-wrapped steering wheel. The list also included luxury carpeting, interior courtesy lighting, wood-grain appliqués, dual illuminated visor mirrors, luxury door and quarter panel trim, and a luxurious cloth-covered split-bench seat with adjustable headrests. All these luxury touches were available for a base price of $15,789.

The most improved model of the 1987 Thunderbird line had to be the Turbo Coupe. Previous Turbo Coupes were fine performance cars in their own right, but they couldn't hold a candle to this new and improved version. The Thunderbird Turbo Coupe was now a world-class performance car.

It still relied on Ford's 2.3-liter overhead cam four-cylinder engine for motivation, and it still featured a Garrett AIResearch Tur-

Even the base model Thunderbird coupe was a handsome car. *Ford Motor Company*

bocharger, but now this engine used an intercooler to help boost its power output. An intercooler is a device which draws in cooler outside air to help boost the turbo's charge. In the case of the five-speed manual transmission version, the addition of an intercooler helped boost the horsepower rating from 155 to 190 at 4600rpm. For the Turbo Coupe equipped with the AOD transmission, the horsepower rating was a slightly more conservative 150. Torque ratings for the five-speed manual cars was 240lb-ft at 3400rpm, while the automatic version came in with a rating of 200lb-ft at 3000rpm.

A more powerful, more torquey engine wasn't the only change seen on the new Turbo Coupes. The potential for greater speed required better braking, in this case supplied by four-wheel anti-lock disc brakes.

Another sophisticated feature found on the 1987 Turbo Coupe was Automatic Ride Control, an interactive system controlled by a module that monitored signals from speed, brake pressure, and steering sensors, as well as an acceleration signal from the EEC-IV engine computer. As this control module reacts to these inputs, it adjusts the shock absorber damping to provide the best ride and handling in all situations. In normal situations, the shock damping tends toward the soft side for good ride quality. But when extra handling capability is required, the shocks auto-

matically adjust to a firm setting. The driver can also select the firm mode manually by flipping a switch on the instrument panel.

Exterior touches also helped set the Turbo Coupe apart from the rest of the Thunderbird line, beginning with the black accent trim. Black paint was applied to the outside door handles, antenna and mounting bezel, lock bezels, window trim, mirrors, and wide body side moldings. The Turbo Coupe also featured a grilleless headlight header panel and a hood with twin intercooler air vents. Underneath this header panel was a unique air dam-type fascia with Hella driving lamps for night driving. Other unique Turbo Coupe features included a red-stripe band encircling the car, Turbo Coupe emblems, and cast-aluminum wheels on P225/60 VR16 black sidewall Goodyear performance radials.

These new Turbo Coupe features were additions to the renowned standard equipment which included articulated sports seats, power windows, luxury carpeting, and luxury door and quarter panel trim.

All this equipment and features made the Thunderbird Turbo Coupe one of the best cars of the 1987 model year—which might explain why the Turbo Coupe was chosen as *Motor Trend*'s Car of the Year for 1987. The best part of the Turbo Coupe deal for 1987 was its base price of $17,032—quite a bargain when you consider that this Thunderbird of-

In hot pink with lots of flashy graphics and a twin-turbocharged 351ci Motorsport V-8 under the hood, this 1988 Thunderbird is one fast-running Pro-Street machine.

fered more equipment than was found on cars costing considerably more.

In addition to this impressive model line-up, Ford offered its customers a little extra to make these cars an even better deal. This extra was called Preferred Equipment Packages, and these packages allowed buyers to load up their cars with popular options at a discounted price compared to the costs of paying for these items separately.

Say a customer ordered Preferred Package 151A, offered to anyone ordering a base

---

1987
Thunderbird, Sport, LX Exterior Colors
Black
Light Grey
Scarlet Red
Sand Beige
Oxford White
Silver*
Medium Grey*
Medium Red*
Silver Blue*
Dark Taupe*
Light Taupe*
Dark Shadow Blue*
Driftwood*
Sandalwood*
*Optional Clearcoat Metallic Colors

Turbo Coupe Exterior Colors
Black
Oxford White
Silver*
Medium Grey*
Medium Red*
Silver Blue*
Dark Shadow Blue*
Driftwood*
*Optional Clearcoat Metallic Colors

Options

5-liter (302ci) EFI V-8 (standard on Sport)	$639
Four-speed AOD transmission (standard on all models except Turbo Coupe)	$515
P215/70R14 whitewall radial tires	$72
Conventional spare tire	$73
Heavy-duty battery (54amp)	$27
Electronic Equipment Group	
Standard Model Thunderbird	$634
Sport and Turbo Coupe	$365
LX	$577
Front floor mats	$30
Luxury Light Convenience Group	
Standard Model Thunderbird	$461
Standard Model with Electronic Equipment Group	$379
Sport and Turbo Coupe	$426
Sport and Turbo Coupe with Electronic Equipment Group	$344
LX	$244

Power antenna	$76
Dual power seats	
LX or Added Value Packages	$302
LX with articulated seats or Added Value Package	$251
Defroster rear window	$145
Immersion engine block heater	$18
Illuminated entry system (standard on LX)	$82
Power Lock Group (standard on LX)	$249
Dual electronic remote control mirrors (standard on LX and Turbo Coupe)	$96
Power moonroof	
Thunderbird, Sport, or Turbo Coupe	$841
LX or Luxury Light Convenience Group	$741
Clearcoat paint	$183
Two-tone paint	
Thunderbird	$218
LX	$163
AM/FM stereo radio Delete Option Credit	$206
Electronic AM/FM stereo with cassette tape player (standard on LX)	$137
Graphic equalizer	$218
Premium sound system	$168
Articulated sports seats (standard on Turbo Coupe)	$183
All-vinyl seat trim	$37
Leather seats	$415
Six-way power driver seat (standard on LX)	$251
Dual power seats (standard on Sport)	
Thunderbird and LX	$554
Turbo Coupe	$502
Speed control (standard on Sport and LX)	$176
Leather-wrapped luxury steering wheel (standard on LX and Sport)	$59
Tilt-Away steering wheel (standard on LX)	$124
Body and decklid stripes (standard on LX)	$55
Body and decklid sports tape combo (Sport, only with 154A Package)	$18
Locking wire wheel covers	
LX or 151A Package	$90
Thunderbird	$212
Cast-aluminum wheels	
LX, Sport, or with 151A Package	$89
Thunderbird	$211
Styled road wheels (standard on Sport or LX)	$122
Power windows (standard on LX and Turbo Coupe)	$222
Intermittent wipers (standard on LX and Turbo Coupe)	$55
California emissions system	$99
High-altitude emission system	No charge

Preferred Packages Options

	T-Bird 151A	Sport 154A	LX 161A	Select LX 162A	Turbo Coupe 157A
Rear window defroster	X	X	X	X	X
Electronic digital clock	X	X	X	X	X
Intermittent wipers	X	X	X	X	X
Light Group	X	X	X	X	X
Power Lock Group	X	X	X	X	X
Dual electric remote control mirrors	X	X	X	X	X
Electronic AM/FM stereo with cassette	X	X	X	X	X
Speed control	X	X	X	X	X
Power driver seat	X	X	X	X	X
Tilt-Away steering wheel	X	X	X	X	X
Power windows	X	X	X	X	X
Body and decklid striping	X	X	X	X	
Styled road wheels	X	X	X	X	
Premium Luxury Package					
Heavy-duty battery			X	X	X
Electronic Equipment Group					X
Front floor mats				X	
Luxury Light/Convenience Group				X	
Power antenna				X	
Dual power seats with power recliners			X		

model Thunderbird. The savings ranged from $770 to $825. Preferred Package 154A saved the Thunderbird Sport buyer $415–$470. The Thunderbird LX customer ordering Preferred Package 161A could save $145. With Preferred Package 162A, also known as the Select LX version, a luxury equipment package, the buyer could save $594. And the Turbo Coupe buyer who ordered Preferred Package 157A could save as much as $1,082.

These packages offered advantages to both Ford Motor Company and Thunderbird buyers. For Ford, it meant that more cars could be built with the same equipment, reducing assembly line time and costs. The company could also make a little extra money that it might not otherwise have made. For the Thunderbird buyer, it meant that they got a better-equipped car at a lower cost.

1988

With all the changes made to the 1987 Thunderbirds, there was little money in the company coffers for major alterations to the 1988 Thunderbirds. The 1988 model year was an interim year for Thunderbirds anyway, with major changes slated for the 1989 Thunderbirds. As in 1988, the Thunderbird buyer was offered four choices: Thunderbird, Thunderbird LX, Thunderbird Sport, and Turbo Coupe.

Chapter 13

1989-1994 Something New and a Blast from the Past

★★★	1989-1992 Thunderbird
★★★★	1989-1993 Thunderbird LX
★★★★	1992 Thunderbird Sport
★★★★	1989-1993 Thunderbird Super Coupe
★★★★★	1990 35th Anniversary Edition Thunderbird

Soon after the sleek new 1983 Thunderbirds hit the streets, work began on its successor. This new Thunderbird project, code-named "MN12," started out as a front-wheel-drive platform. Halfway through the design and development stages, Ford decided to change the platform to the more traditional rear-wheel-drive system found on all Thunderbirds.

One of the main reasons that a front-wheel-drive system was even considered was that Ford was then working on the Taurus/Sable program and thought it might save some money by using the same platform for the Thunderbird, too. With the change in direction, however, the two platforms shared very little in common.

Like its predecessors, the new MN12 Thunderbird spent considerable time in the

wind tunnel. Some 700 hours were logged this time around. The time was well spent, as the new standard model Thunderbird and the Thunderbird LX scored a coefficient of drag rating of 0.31.

1989

The new-for-1989 Thunderbird featured a longer wheelbase and a wider stance on a new floor platform. The wheelbase increased

As you can see here, the 1989 Thunderbirds were extensively redesigned. From front to back, top to bottom, they didn't share anything with the 1988 models they replaced. *Ford Motor Company*

The Thunderbird Super Coupe featured a unique front fascia, wheels, and ground-effects side skirts. *Ford Motor Company*

126

by 9in, though the overall length of the new Thunderbird decreased by 3in. Front tread was increased by 3.3in, while the rear tread was widened by 1.7in. Moving the wheels farther apart helped improve the Thunderbird's handling characteristics, and the longer wheelbase provided for more interior space and a better ride.

A new feature on the Thunderbird's underside that helped it handle better was a new independent rear suspension, a first for the Thunderbird. Independent front and rear suspension gave the Thunderbird some sports car handling characteristics.

There were just as many new features found on the car's exterior as there were underneath. From front to rear, top to bottom, the new car really stood out from the old, with a new roof design and redesigned fenders, doors, trunk lid, hood, and front and rear fascias. The headlights, taillights, grille, trim, mirrors, and wheels were all changed. Changes were also made throughout the interior.

In the mid-1980s when the new Thunderbird concept was starting to take shape, the general consensus around Detroit was that the V-8 engine was on its last legs. Some people also thought that a four-cylinder engine shouldn't be used in a Thunderbird—even a great engine such as the turbocharged four-cylinder. Because of this reasoning, the only

In these photos, we can see that there really wasn't too much difference between the 1989 and 1990 models. *Ford Motor Company*

engine planned for the new Thunderbird was the 3.8-liter (232ci) V-6. By specifying only one engine, the Ford designers and package planners could work with a smaller engine compartment box, which allowed the hood line of the new cars to be set at a lower height, thus producing a sleeker-looking package.

The 35th Anniversary Thunderbird was really something special, from its unique exterior paint scheme to its commemorative badges. *Ford Motor Company*

127

These sleek new Thunderbirds made their public debut on December 26, 1988. Three models were available: the Thunderbird, Thunderbird LX, and the new Thunderbird Super Coupe.

In standard form, the Thunderbird came pretty well equipped, with such items as factory air conditioning, tinted glass, power rack and pinion steering, independent rear suspension, intermittent wipers, motorized shoulder restraints, 3.8-liter V-6 with sequential electronic fuel injection, four-speed AOD transmission, and lap belts and shoulder restraints for the outside rear seat passengers.

In addition to the standard items found in the base Thunderbird, the Thunderbird LX came equipped with an electronic instrument cluster, AM/FM stereo radio with cassette

Once again, hardly any exterior changes were made to the 1991 Thunderbirds to help distinguish them from the similar 1990 models. *Ford Motor Company*

Shown here is a 1992 Thunderbird Sport which, like the LX model, now had a front fascia treatment similar to the Super Coupe version. *Ford Motor Company*

tape player, leather-wrapped steering wheel, six-way power driver seat, power locks, vehicle maintenance monitor, and Tilt-Away steering wheel.

The last 1989 model available in the Thunderbird lineup was the Thunderbird Super Coupe, which replaced the Turbo Coupe as the high-performance model. It featured a 215hp, supercharged, and intercooled 3.8-liter V-6 engine; dual exhausts; four-wheel disc brakes; an anti-lock braking system; handling suspension with automatic ride control; 16in cast-aluminum wheels; high-performance radial tires; Traction-Lok rear axle; articulated sports seats; a five-speed manual overdrive transmission (a four-speed automatic was available at an extra cost); unique front and rear fascia treatments; and side aerodynamic sports skirting.

Soon after the Super Coupe was released, it was chosen as *Motor Trend*'s Car of the Year for 1989, a worthy honor for such a fine car. About the same time Ford was making a big deal about winning this prestigious award, it discovered a batch of weak crankshafts in the company's supply of engines; a major problem for the Super Coupe. These crankshafts probably would have worked with no problems when used in a base Thunderbird or LX model, but when exposed to the additional stress imposed by an Eaton supercharger the possibility of failure was very real. So Ford

stopped producing and distributing these cars until this problem could be remedied, and put a hold and recall on any cars already in the pipeline.

1990

Changes in the 1990 Thunderbird were minimal because Ford had spent so much money developing the 1989 models. The lineup was the same as it was in 1989, consisting of the base Thunderbird, the LX, and the Super Coupe.

1990
35th Anniversary Edition Features
Black and Titanium two-tone paint
Blue accent stripes
Commemorative fender badges and unique
    Thunderbird emblems
Black-finished road wheels
Special grey suede cloth seats with black leather
    bolsters
Fold-down rear split-bench seat
Commemorative badges on door panels
210hp supercharged and intercooled V-6 engine
Dual exhausts
Four-wheel disc brakes
Traction-Lok rear axle
Articulated sports seats
Performance analog instrumentation
Five-speed manual/overdrive transmission
Optional four-speed AOD transmission

These two photos of 1993 Thunderbirds show only some exterior trim upgrades over the 1992 versions. *Ford Motor Company*

This was the 35th anniversary of the Thunderbird, and once again, Ford dished up a nice surprise for those who wanted a unique Thunderbird. Called the 35th Anniversary Edition, it was based on the Super Coupe. The most striking feature found on this special model was its special black and titanium (silver) paint. This black-and-silver combination was carried over to the interior, with black leather side bolsters framing special gray suede cloth seats. This special model was available on a limited-production basis, with only about 5,000 cars produced.

1991

Once again for 1991, model year changes were kept to a minimum. The standard base model Thunderbird got an upgraded luxury cloth interior, the LX got some leather accents on its seats and vinyl and cloth inserts on its door panels, and the Super Coupe received some embroidered Thunderbird emblems on the seat backs.

Bowing to popular demand, Ford again offered a V-8 option for the Thunderbird and Thunderbird LX models. This was the same engine offered in the 5.0-liter Mustang, but a more cramped engine compartment forced Ford to redesign some parts so that the engine would fit. Unfortunately, those redesigned parts tended to rob the engine of some of its power. In the Mustang, this 302ci V-8 put out 225hp, whereas in the Thunderbird, it was rated at only 200hp—higher than the base V-6 but lower than the Super Coupe's 210hp rating.

From a rear 3/4 view, the 1994 Thunderbird doesn't look that much different from Thunderbirds produced from 1989 to 1993. All the noticeable changes were made to the car's front end. *Ford Motor Company*

1992

The Thunderbird Sport returned to the lineup in 1992. The Sport was basically a regular Thunderbird with a 200hp 5.0-liter V-8 sitting under the hood. Other Thunderbirds offered in 1992 were the base Thunderbird, LX, and Super Coupe.

The biggest change seen in the 1992 Thunderbird lineup involved the non-Super Coupe models. For the first time, all Thunderbird models shared an aerodynamic front end similar to that on the Super Coupe. Now, all Thunderbirds looked alike, or at least similar, from a distance.

Other new features for 1992 included color-keyed body side moldings; a new, full-width taillight lit by LEDs; and some interior changes.

1993

The base Thunderbird and Thunderbird Sport models were dropped for the 1993 model year, leaving only the Thunderbird LX and the Super Coupe available for buyers this year.

The LX was equipped with a special package featuring electronic temperature and air conditioning controls, cast-aluminum wheels, a power antenna, color-keyed exterior mirrors, a color-keyed steering wheel, and a leather-wrapped shift knob.

The LX buyer this year could choose between the standard V-6 engine or the optional 5.0-liter V-8. The Super Coupe still boasted a 210hp supercharged V-6, anti-lock brakes, Traction-Lok rear axle adjustable suspension, an electronic AM/FM stereo with cassette

The 1994 Thunderbird features a redesigned interior that shows a lot of Continental Mark VIII influences. The new Thunderbirds also feature dual air bags as standard equipment. *Ford Motor Company*

The most striking exterior change found on the 1994 Thunderbird is a redesigned front end featuring a new grille slot and a revamped fascia panel. *Ford Motor Company*

tape player, and four-wheel disc brakes. Speed-sensitive rack and pinion steering, air conditioning, tinted glass, and power windows were standard equipment on both models.

1994

Ford started production of its 1994 models in August 1993. These new models may look like their 1993 predecessors from a distance, but once you get up close, you'll see several changes. You'll notice a new hood design, new headlamps, new bumpers, and other exterior modifications. The exterior changes pale in comparison to the interior updates. Ford completely redesigned the interior to make it more user friendly to both driver and passengers. The dashboard layout now features a twin-pod cockpit design. On the driver's side, the instrument cluster, analog gauges, and controls are placed close to hand and seem to wrap around the driver. Everything is easier to reach and read, making for a more pleasing driving experience. For an increased margin of interior safety, twin airbags are fitted for the driver and the front seat passenger, and the seat belts feature a new three-point setup that replaces the passive, motorized system used previously.

In following the latest environmental trends, the air conditioning systems are now CFC-free. Other changes inside these cars include cup holders located in the console, illuminated door switches, a new steering wheel, and an upgraded stereo with built-in CD changer. There's even a "hands-off" cellular telephone available.

Once again there are two Thunderbird models from which to choose. The base model LX is priced at $16,380, and the Super Coupe starts at $23,000. Both cars are equipped with 3.8-liter V-6s, the LX's making 140hp while the Super Coupe pumps an impressive 230hp.

If the base LX provides too little power for your tastes, but the Super Coupe offers too much, you might want to consider the LX with Ford's new 4.6-liter modular V-8 option. This engine makes 205hp and 265lb-ft of torque at 3200rpm at a cost of $515.

Ford cut the price of the Thunderbird in 1993 and sales jumped by 44,000 units over 1992. Ford is committed to keeping the Thunderbird's cost at a level where more people can afford it.

In 1995 or 1996, a new Thunderbird will make its debut. Watch closely to see what the future brings. Rumors floating around now say it could be either a front-wheel-drive or a rear-wheel-drive car. There is also talk that these cars will have more powerful engines and some design traits to really set it apart from the latest Thunderbirds.

Chapter 14

Thunder Birds

For most of its history, Ford's Thunderbird has been an automobile of distinction, a car with touches of luxury that appeals to people who want to be pampered.

When the Thunderbird was first introduced as a two-seater in 1954, some people thought of it as a sports car even though Ford promoted it as a sporty personal car. Some people even modified the Thunderbird into a racing car. In stock form, from a competition perspective, the Thunderbird left much to be desired, but when modified properly, it didn't do too badly.

Ford got back into racing on a full-time basis with its own factory teams in 1956, and modified Thunderbirds were part of the company's racing efforts. Factory racing Thunderbirds were found at places like Daytona, Sebring, Bonneville, and other racing venues. They managed to set some records and win a race or two, but they didn't set the racing world on fire. By contrast, Chevrolet pulled

A lone Thunderbird racer battles a group of Chevrolets at a NASCAR race in the late-1970s. *David Allio*

One of Bill Elliott's Thunderbird race cars now spends a much quieter life on display in the Henry Ford Museum.

out all the stops to take Corvettes racing, and it played up any wins the Corvette teams recorded, advertising these wins on radio and television and in newspapers and magazines.

In the more important sales race, however, the Corvette was a distant second to the Thunderbird, and word around Detroit was that if the Corvette didn't start scoring some high numbers on the sales charts, it would be history. But with each race, the Corvette got a little better, and the start of a legend was born.

Ford came back again in 1957 with a full-fledged factory racing assault which lasted until the Automobile Manufacturers Associa-

tion voted to adopt a "no racing/performance promotion" position. For all intents and purposes, Ford was out of racing.

By the time the Thunderbird grew into a four-seater automobile for 1958, the Ford Motor Company had forsaken racing activities of all sorts, so the possibility of a factory-based racing Thunderbird seemed rather remote. However, in 1959 when it seemed that all the other manufacturers were actively involved in racing and performance promotions, the Ford Motor Company decided to again test the racing waters. Because Ford wanted to use the largest engine available in its lineup, the Thunderbird with its optional 430ci pow-

BUDDY BAKER
Wood Brothers Thunderbird

DICK BROOKS
Donlavey Chameleon Thunderbird

BILL ELLIOTT
Coors Melling Thunderbird

KYLE PETTY
7-Eleven Petty Enterprises

RICKY RUDD
Bud Moore Wrangler Thunderbird

Ford
MOTORSPORT

1984

NASCAR WINSTON CUP SERIES

In 1984, Ford had quite an impressive roster of drivers running Thunderbirds in NASCAR's Winston Cup Series. *Ford Motorsport*

Brooks Racing ran this Thunderbird in IMSA's GTO Series in 1984. John Bauer was driving this car when it was photographed. *Ford Motorsport*

The Wood Brothers Racing Team, Ford race car constructors since the mid-1950s, prepared this Thunderbird for Kyle Petty who was their driver back in the mid-1980s. *Ford Motorsport*

erplant was chosen to carry the Ford racing banner. Holman & Moody, a racing shop based in Charlotte, North Carolina, prepared some cars, and Ford was back in racing. These Thunderbird racers did quite well, one even coming within a whisker of winning the 1959 Daytona 500, stock car racing's premiere event. By the time the 1959 racing season was over, Thunderbirds had won six stock car races on the NASCAR circuit—quite a perfor-

mance for a car that was not considered racy in any way, shape, or form.

The next Thunderbird/racing tie-in occurred in 1961, when a new, gold-colored 1961 Thunderbird convertible was chosen to pace the Golden Anniversary Edition of the Indy 500 Race.

From then until 1977, there would be hardly any connection between racing and Ford's Thunderbirds. The Thunderbird was now aimed at the luxury/personal market, and with each passing year the Thunderbird moved farther away from the performance scene. That all changed in 1977, because Ford needed a new car to carry the performance

A NASCAR Thunderbird leads a pack of GM racers during a stock car race in 1984. *Ford Motorsport*

This modified Thunderbird is part of the PPG Racing Pace Car Fleet. You'll see Thunderbirds like this pacing races throughout the United States.

BOB GLIDDEN

Motorcraft *Racing*
PRO STOCK
THUNDERBIRD

Thunderbirds make pretty good drag racers, too. Bob Glidden has run several Thunderbird Pro Stock cars and won races and championships with them. *Ford Motorsport*

banner in stock car racing, and the new lighter, mid-size Thunderbird body fit the bill perfectly. At the hands of such drivers as Bobby Allison, Dick Brooks, and Jody Ridley, these Thunderbirds would once again visit victory lane.

In the late-1970s, everybody was getting on the "smaller is better" bandwagon—and that included NASCAR, who ruled in 1980 that starting in the 1981 season, auto manufacturers would be allowed to run smaller bodies in the Winston Cup Series for stock cars. Like the GM teams that raced the smaller Chevrolet Monte Carlo, Pontiac Grand Prix, and Buick bodies, Ford decided to stay in racing with its smaller Thunderbird body. Even though these new Thunderbirds had the aerodynamics of a brick, they managed to win their fair share of races and keep Ford in the thick of competition.

What really helped the Thunderbird's racing cause was the introduction in late-1982 of the "aero look" 1983 Thunderbirds. When the Ford teams showed up at Daytona with their new Thunderbird racing cars, the GM racers screamed "foul," and NASCAR started to formulate rules changes that would keep the Thunderbirds from dominating the Winston Cup Series. Although the Thunderbirds were winning more races, they weren't dominating the sport. After all, they were outnumbered by the GM forces, and the parts the GM teams were using were better developed and stronger than the parts the Ford teams were using. There were many parts failures back then, and unfortunately the cars that were breaking down were Thunderbirds. When the Thunderbirds were running strong, however, there was nobody that could beat them.

Despite these hardships, Ford teams persevered and finally, in 1985, everything started to come together—especially the Coors/Melling team and its "No. 9 Thunderbird," a car driven by "Awesome Bill from Dawsonville" Elliott. That year, Elliott was unstoppable, winning eleven consecutive races and receiving the "Winston Million" for winning three major races over 500 miles in one season. After that performance, the threat of Thunderbird dominance in NASCAR became a distinct possibility. So for 1986, NASCAR issued a new set of rules that made the GM cars almost as aerodynamic as the Thunderbirds.

Thunderbirds were winning in other racing arenas. Bob Glidden was dominating NHRA drag racing's Pro Stock class in a 1983 Thunderbird, and the same thing was happening in IHRA Pro Stock competition. Thunderbirds were also racing and winning in the IMSA GTO Series for sports coupes. In fact, Thunderbirds were winning so many races now that people started thinking of them as performance cars rather than luxomobiles.

Under Ford's Motorsport/SVO Racing Program of the mid-1980s, the racing Thunderbirds were getting better with each and every race they entered. And as their racing successes started to build, other teams dropped their GM cars and switched over to the Ford camp—which meant that the chances of winning in a Ford were getting better all the time.

For example, consider Bill Elliott who has been in a Ford stock car since the beginning of his racing career. In 1982, he won his first NASCAR Winston Cup race. Six years later, he won NASCAR's Driving Championship, driving a Thunderbird. Other drivers who have received glory in Thunderbird race cars are Davey Allison, Cale Yarborough, Geoff

Thunderbird racers like this one even race up the sides of mountains during the annual Pike's Peak Auto Hill Climb.

Bodine, Mark Martin, Rickey Rudd, Morgan Shepherd, Kyle Petty, and Dale Earnhardt. That's quite a list of impressive driving talent.

The Thunderbird's best year for NASCAR Winston Cup racing had to be 1992, when the Thunderbirds so dominated the series that Ford walked away with NASCAR's Manufacturer's Cup. It was the first time Ford had won that honor since 1969.

What do all these racing activities and wins mean to the average Thunderbird enthusiast? The Thunderbird's rich racing heritage and greater exposure in the automotive arena, translates into more sales and more Thunderbird enthusiasts to share in the Thunderbird legacy.

Thunderbird Collectibles

Like most Americans at the time, I thought the 1955 Thunderbird was the most beautiful car that had ever come out of Detroit. I would have loved to own one in 1955, but I had a problem. At seven years old, I could neither buy nor drive one.

The PowerCar Company of Mystic, Connecticut, had a solution to this problem: a scaled-down version of the full-sized Thunderbird, called the Thunderbird Jr., that was just the right size for a child of my age. It had a realistic-looking fiberglass body draped over a steel frame, and was available in two forms, one pedal-powered like a bicycle and the other propelled by a 6-volt electric motor The motor supplied with this second version was a 6-volt starter like the one used on a full-sized Thunderbird. The cost of the motor-dri-

ven Thunderbird Jr. was $395, and the pedal car version could be had for $298. These prices seem reasonable by today's standards, but they were quite high in 1955. Not many parents could afford to buy their kids a Thunderbird Jr., which might explain why so few of them were sold back in the 1950s and why they are hard to find today.

The PowerCar Company made the Thunderbird Jr. available for twelve years, from 1955 through 1967. Each year when the new Thunderbirds would arrive, a new Thunderbird Jr. would be released (except for 1967, when the 1966 model was used). Costs ranged from a low of $298 for a pedal-powered 1955 model to a high of $597 for a 3hp Briggs & Stratton-powered 1966 model in 1967.

Thunderbird Jr.'s show up at swap meets every now and then. If you should run across

A proud young man cruises a California car show in his Thunderbird Jr. in 1984.

A Thunderbird Jr. on display beside one of its larger brothers. Doesn't this combination make for an eye-catching display?

Here are some other 35th anniversary Thunderbird mementos.

Magazine ads, such as this full-color one from 1955, make nice paper collectibles.

one, consider yourself lucky and be prepared to pay handsomely for it. If you don't want to buy an old, worn-out version, Jeff Van-derZanden in Wisconsin is advertising rebuilt Thunderbird Jr.'s for $2,995. These exact reproductions are replicas of the 1955, 1956, or 1957 PowerCar originals. Be it an original PowerCar Thunderbird Jr. or one of these reproductions, either one will make a nice addition to any Thunderbird collection.

If a Thunderbird Jr. is too rich for your budget, you might want to start a collection of Thunderbird promotional models or model car kits. At least one Thunderbird promotional model was available for each model year from 1955 through 1971. AMT was the first to offer a Thunderbird promotional model of the 1955 version in the winter of 1954, and it was probably the last company to produce a Thunderbird promotional model when the last one was released in 1971. If you do decide to get involved with collecting Thunderbird promotionals, be advised that they don't come cheap. Depending on condition and rarity, a Thunderbird promotional model can

cost from $30 to almost $300—compared to the $15.80 your Ford dealer paid for a dozen such models in 1956. On another note, the red 1957 Thunderbird promotional seems to be the easiest one to find today, perhaps because of a 1957 promotional campaign when Ford sent out thousands of these models to customers and potential customers.

Thunderbird model car kits might be a little easier to find and a little cheaper since

This miniature 1962 Thunderbird is a promotional model issued in 1962.

Solido has a very nice die-cast rendition of a 1961 Thunderbird convertible in 1/43rd scale.

Even dolls get to ride around in Thunderbirds.

demand doesn't seem to be as high. From the late-1950s through the late-1960s, several Thunderbird models were available, especially in kit form. Most of these models were annual releases that accompanied introductions of their real-car counterparts. Most of these kits have been out of production for many years, so you'll have to look for them at swap meets, through antique toy dealers, or through dealers who specialize in models. Some models are still available through toy stores and hobby shops, two of the more popular being AMT's 1957 Thunderbird and Monogram's 1958. Also available are kits of late-model Thunderbirds and Thunderbird NASCAR racers.

Several nice die-cast Thunderbird models have been released the last few years. Revell has some fine 1955 and 1956 Thunderbirds available in 1/18 scale as part of its Scale Masterpiece Series. Other recent die-cast Thunderbird releases have come from Dinky, Brooklin, Solido, and the Franklin Mint.

Back in the mid-1950s and early-1960s, the Post Cereal Company included small plastic models of cars, trucks, boats, and Greyhound buses with their products. These cars were molded in colorful plastic by the F&F Moldworks in Ohio and were models of Fords and Mercurys of that period. In 1954, some cereal boxes contained a model of a 1955 Thunderbird with the Fairlane-style trim found on a few early Thunderbirds; a plain-looking 1955 model, without this extra trim,

A 1959 Thunderbird Jr. is shown on display in front of Ford's World Headquarters in Dearborn, Michigan.

This model of a 1966 Thunderbird is a reissue of the original kit that was released as an annual in 1966.

This little 1959 Thunderbird hardtop, molded by the F&F Mold Works, came out of a Post Company cereal box in 1959.

was the included prize in 1955; and 1959 cereal boxes contained a hardtop or convertible model. The next Thunderbird models appeared in specially marked Post boxes in 1961 and 1962, when lucky cereal eaters could find a hardtop, convertible, or Sports Roadster (1962). These cars may have been carried over into 1963 also.

Several toy car Thunderbirds made of tin, rubber, and plastic were also released from 1955 through the early-1970s. In 1972, for instance, Proctor and Gamble placed some toy cars in boxes of detergent. One of these "soap box cars" was a 1971-1972 Thunderbird hardtop. Out-of-production toy cars like these can

be found at swap meets or at toy shows held around the country.

Another Thunderbird collectible worthy of mention here is showroom catalogs. These beautiful full-color catalogs contain much useful information for the Thunderbird enthusiast. Some of these catalogs are works of art, with gallery-quality photography used throughout. In addition to these catalogs there are shop manuals and parts books, which are not only collectibles, but will also help you with your restorations. Factory promotional postcards mailed to prospective Thunderbird customers and magazine advertisements are other possible collectibles.

In honor of the 25th, 30th, and 35th anniversaries of the Thunderbird, Ford prepared all sorts of promotional and commemorative materials, including historical booklets,

Although this box is well worn from more than thirty years of handling, the unbuilt model kit contained inside is still in remarkable condition.

This 1960 Thunderbird hardtop is a promotional model that was given away by a Ford dealer in 1960.

Thunderbird jewelry circa 1964, as it appeared in a catalog sent to Ford salesmen.

In 1968, AMT used some nice box art on its annual kits. There are collectors today who collect only the boxes because they like the artwork so much.

decals, patches, pins, and hats. Any of these items would make a good addition to any collection.

In years past, Ford customers could buy all sorts of Thunderbird-related materials, including rings, bracelets, cuff links, tie bars, glasses, notebooks, and key fobs. These items are very valuable now, especially if they are period pieces, and will make nice additions to any Thunderbird collection.

Over the last few years, Ford's motorsport apparel catalogs have displayed Thunderbird items that can be bought and used now or saved as a future collectible. These items include shirts, ties, cuff links, hats, pins, badges, sweaters, belts, and belt buckles. Chances are, if an item has a Thunderbird crest on it, it will be collected by Thunderbird aficionados in the future.

Thunderbird Promotional Models

1955 convertible, top down: in Torch Red, Thunderbird Blue, White, Waterfall Blue, Neptune Green, Raven Black
1956 convertible, top down: Raven Black, Fiesta Red, Buckskin Tan, Peacock Blue, Colonial White, Thunderbird Green, Meadowmist Green, Diamond Blue
1957 convertible, top down: Red, Pink, Green
1958 hardtop
1959 hardtop or convertible, with or without flywheel motor: Various colors
1960 hardtop and convertible models
1961 hardtop and convertible models
1962 hardtop, convertible, Sports Roadster
1963 hardtop, convertible, Sports Roadster
1964 hardtop, convertible, and radio-equipped models
1964 Thunderbird promotionals were equipped with a Philco transistor radio): Burgundy, Rangoon Red, White, Black, Pagoda Green
1966 Landau hardtop: Arcadian Blue, Candyapple Red, Bronze, Burgundy, Tahoe Turquoise, White
1967 hardtop and radio-equipped models: Frost Turquoise, White, Red, Light Green
1968 hardtop: Various colors
1969 hardtop and radio-equipped models available: Various colors
1970 hardtop
1971 hardtop

Chapter 16

Specials, One-Offs, Reproductions, and Odd 'Birds

No Thunderbird book would be complete without some mention of Thunderbirds and Thunderbird-related vehicles that fall outside of the regular-production realm. In this chapter, we'll review some of these lesser-known Thunderbirds.

The first example of a special one-off styling exercise that affected Thunderbirds of the future was a Ford Design Studio dream car called the X-100. This car made its debut in the mid-1950s and included many futuristic touches that would be seen on later Fords,

Lincolns, and Mercurys. For instance, the X-100 featured quarter panels and taillights that looked like jet engine pods and would appear on 1961–1963 Ford Thunderbirds. Another X-100 feature found on Thunderbirds was its use of wide roof C panels. These wide roof panels would be a Thunderbird trademark, appearing on cars from 1958 through 1982.

Restyling stock-looking cars into customs was all the rage in the United States, starting in 1956 and continuing through 1967. One famous customizer was George Barris, who in

Several features of Ford's mid-1950s X-100 dream car ended up on future Thunderbirds. *Ford Motor Company*

The *Italien* was a really slick-looking Thunderbird show car that came out of the Ford Design Studios in 1963. *Ford Motor Company*

1961 modified a 1961 Thunderbird convertible into a full-sized rendition of the "Styline" Thunderbird. The Styline Series of plastic car models was introduced by AMT. The beauty of these kits was that a modeler could take a model of a stock-looking car and transform it into a dream car. One of the most popular kits in the series was the 1961 Thunderbird hardtop. Barris wanted to show that the customized model created in the kit could easily be reproduced on a real car, so he transformed a real version for AMT's vice-president, George Toteff. The car was originally painted a bright red but a year or so later it

was repainted in Lime Metallic Custom and dubbed the "Hairy Canary." It was then taken on the custom car show circuit by the "Katt from AMT," Budd Anderson. The Hairy Canary was a popular fixture in the Ford Custom Car Caravan. A now-rusty Hairy Canary awaits a future restoration, and someday, we may see this famous car again on the car show circuit.

Another Ford Custom Caravan car that was very popular at that time was a styling/customizing effort done by the Ford Design Studio called the *Italien*. This car was basically a regular 1963 Thunderbird convertible to

Here's a 1959 Thunderbird styling exercise with a special "pop-up" roof panel. *Ford Motor Company*

which was affixed a special fastback roofline. This roofline, about as different as one could get from that of the regular, square Thunderbird, changed the looks of the car dramatically. Fastback rooflines were popular on Fords then, and it's a shame the company never put an *Italien*-styled Thunderbird into production. It probably would have sold like the proverbial hotcakes.

Other Thunderbird show cars that came out of the Ford Design Studio in the 1960s included a customized 1964 Thunderbird hardtop called The Golden Palomino, a customized hardtop in 1967 called the Apollo, and the Saturn and Saturn II modifications of a 1968 and 1969 hardtop, respectively. The Apollo actually made it into limited production in 1967, but because of its enormous expense, only five were produced.

In 1960, the Allegheny-Ludlum Steel Company wanted to promote the use of stainless steel in automotive production, and it devised a clever idea for a promotion involving the Thunderbird. Allegheny-Ludlum approached the Budd Company, which supplied all of Ford's Thunderbird bodies from 1954 through 1960, and asked that company to put together a special Thunderbird body which would look like a regular 1960 Thun-

Is a copy really "the sincerest form of flattery?" This Shay Reproduction 1955 'Bird is a nice replica.

derbird body except it would be made entirely of stainless steel. It was an expensive proposition, but Allegheny-Ludlum wanted to create the ultimate Thunderbird show car. The plan succeeded in spades; the 1960 Stainless Steel Thunderbird in its buffed, stainless-steel patina, was a show stopper wherever it went. Thousands of Americans saw it on its national promotional tour in 1960, and thousands more will see it in the year 2000 when it comes out of retirement to recreate that tour. The amazing thing about this car is that it will

This promotional postcard shows the Allegheny Ludlum stainless-steel Thunderbird—a very unique car to say the least.

The *Apollo* was a Thunderbird show car that actually made it into very limited production (only five were built). *Ford Motor Company*

look exactly the same as it did forty years ago, because stainless steel has natural properties that overcome the ravages of time. Next to a regular 1960 Thunderbird, this car will look like it just stepped off the assembly line. In fact, it was the last 1960 Thunderbird to go down the Wixom, Michigan, assembly line in 1960.

Some people like the looks of the classic Thunderbird but want all the amenities that a more modern car possesses, a modern version of the 1955 Thunderbird, if you will. To satisfy those folks, Harry Shay, in 1979, came up with the idea of reproducing the classic 1955 Thunderbird. Although a Thunderbird purist might cringe at the thought, these cars do have a place in the Thunderbird scheme of things. They are for "non-car people," or car people who don't want to be bothered with going out and finding an original Thunderbird to buy and restore.

As far as reproductions go, Harry Shay's Silver Anniversary Limited Edition models

This show car, called the Saturn, came out of the Ford Design Studios in the late-1960s. *Ford Motor Company*

The Saturn II followed the original Saturn and came out in 1968. *Ford Motor Company*

were pretty nice. They had to be; otherwise, Ford Motor Company would not have given him permission to distribute them through its dealers. Ford is pretty particular when it comes to quality and tie-ins with its name. This reproduction was an exact copy of the 1955 original; except instead of using a steel body, the Shay cars used a body made out of fiberglass, which was mounted on a frame that was a reproduction of the original X-type found under the early Thunderbirds. Powertrain choices included a turbocharged Ford four-cylinder, a Ford V-6, or Ford's fine 302ci V-8.

These Shay reproduction Thunderbirds were built in assembly plants in Wixom and Battle Creek, Michigan, as a turnkey operation. Harry Shay was a stickler for quality assembly work, so he didn't offer any kits for people to assemble themselves. In 1980, one of these 1955 Thunderbird replicas cost $8,950, about the same price as an original 1955 Thunderbird in good condition was bringing at that time.

For Ford performance fans, the name Roush Racing should have a familiar ring. Jack Roush and his company have been building winning racing Fords for many years. In 1986, Roush Inc., under its Mexican subsidiary, ECS Mexicana, entered the car market with its own, limited-edition Thunderbirds for the Mexican market. These cars featured turbocharged 165hp V-6 engines, special BBS 15x8in aluminum wire wheels, Goodyear VR50/225 (front) and VR50/245 (rear) tires, a special ground effects package, and a rear deck spoiler. ECS Mexican called these cars Mexican Grand Prix Thunderbirds, and 1,000 were scheduled to be built for the Mexican market.

A racing tie-in with Thunderbird was also the impetus behind the production of a limited-edition Thunderbird built in Dahlonega, Georgia, called the Bill Elliott Ford Signature Edition Thunderbird. These $18,995 specials were available only through Bill Elliott Ford in Dahlonega, Georgia, or Hardy Family Ford in Dallas, Georgia. Several of these cars were sold to Bill Elliott fans in the southeast.

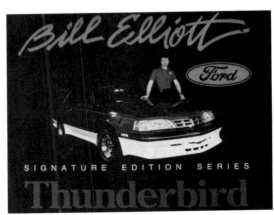

Bill Elliott got into the specialty car business by selling some of these Bill Elliott Signature Edition Thunderbirds.

This special edition Thunderbird built by ECS/Roush Inc. is called the Mexican Grand Prix Thunderbird. It was released in 1986.

They were basically Thunderbird LXs equipped with 302ci V-8 engines, four-speed AOD transmissions, a unique front air dam and rear spoiler, aerodynamic ground effects, and unique aluminum road wheels mounted

A new Thunderbird Super Coupe undergoing the first stage of "short wheelbase" (SWB) modifications in the Auto Kraft facility in Lincoln, Nebraska.

with a set of Firestone SS performance radials. What made these cars stand out, though, was their paint jobs. These Thunderbirds were painted a bright red over a white with gold striping, just like Bill Elliott's #9 Coors Racing Thunderbird.

Have you ever thought that a modern version of the classic two-seater Thunderbird would be a nice thing to park in your garage? A car that combines the looks and performance of the latest Thunderbird Super Coupe with the close-coupled personality of the early Thunderbirds?

If you have dreamed this dream, you might want to contact Kenny Brown at Project Industries in Omaha, Nebraska, or Doug Kielian at Auto Kraft in Lincoln, Nebraska. Both men are involved in building a short-wheelbase Thunderbird, the actual modifications taking place at Auto Kraft.

In a nutshell, the Thunderbird's wheelbase is cut down from 113in to 105in, but there is much more involved than just cutting away 8in of material between the rear of the door and the wheelhouse. A series of cuts are made so that when the body is rejoined, only Kielian knows where the surgical cuts were

From the front, the SWB Thunderbird looks like a regular production Thunderbird that has been personalized with a different hood, wheels, and aero kit.

made. It takes a lot of careful cutting and precise fitting to make sure that this modification looks as clean as if the factory had done it.

Actually, the idea of a short wheelbase Thunderbird originated at Ford Motor Company, where, in 1991, a Thunderbird concept car was built to test the feasibility of using a shortened Thunderbird platform for the next generation of Mustangs. The idea was shelved because the end result was too heavy and too expensive to meet requirements.

Although Ford abandoned this idea, it has worked out well for Brown and Kielian. If you have about $46,000, they can build a short wheelbase Thunderbird for you. And if you like the idea of a convertible Thunderbird, Auto Kraft is planning a short wheelbase Thunderbird Roadster for the future.

The shortened wheelbase of the SWB Thunderbird is most evident when viewed from the rear, as in this shot. Note how the rear roof pillar treatment was changed as part of this modification.

Chassis Specifications

1955 Thunderbird
  Wheelbase: 102in
  Overall length: 175.3in
  Overall width: 70.3in
  Front tread: 56in
  Rear tread: 56in
  Curb weight: 2,980lb
  Tires: 6.70x15in four-ply

1956 Thunderbird
  Wheelbase: 102in
  Overall length: 185in (including Continental
    kit)
  Overall width: 70.3in
  Front tread: 56in
  Rear tread: 56in

1957 Thunderbird
  Wheelbase: 102in
  Overall length: 181.4in
  Front tread: 56in
  Rear tread: 56in
  Height: 51.6in
  Tires: 7.5x14 tubeless
  Steering gear ratio: 23:1
  Rear end ratios:
    Fordomatic transmission 3.10:1
    Conventional three-speed manual 3.56:1
    Overdrive 3.70:1

1958–1960 Thunderbird
  Wheelbase: 113in
  Overall length: 205.4in
  Overall width: 77in
  Height: 52.5in
  Front tread: 60in
  Rear tread: 57in
  Curb weight: 3,708–3,903lb

1961–1963 Thunderbird
  Wheelbase: 113in
  Overall length: 205in
  Overall width: 75.9in
  Height:
    Hardtop: 52.5in
    Convertible: 53.5in
  Curb weight:
    Hardtop: 3,958lb
    Convertible: 4,130lb

1964–1966 Thunderbird
  Wheelbase: 113.2in
  Overall length: 205.4in
  Overall width: 77.1in
  Front tread: 61in
  Rear tread: 60in
  Height
    Hardtop: 52.5in
    Landau: 52.6in
    Convertible: 53.3in
  Curb weight:
    Hardtop: 4,440lb
    Convertible: 4,590lb

1967–1969 Thunderbird
  Wheelbase:
    Two-door: 115in
    Four-door: 117in
  Overall length:
    Two-door: 206.9in
    Four-door: 209.4in
  Width: 77.3in
  Height:
    Two-door: 52.8inches
    Four-door: 53.8in
  Curb Weight:
    Two-door: 4,339–4,445lb

Two-door Landau: 4,453–4,549lb
Four-door Landau: 4,545–4,649lb

1970–1971 Thunderbird
    Wheelbase:
        Two-door: 115in
        Four-door: 117in
    Overall length:
        Two-door: 212.5in
        Four-door: 215in
    Overall width:
        Two-door: 78in
        Four-door: 77.4in
    Height: 51in
    Front tread: 62in
    Rear tread: 62in
    Curb weight: 4,545lb

1972 Thunderbird
    Wheelbase: 120.4in
    Overall length: 216in
    Overall width: 79.3in
    Height: 52.1in
    Front tread: 63in
    Rear tread: 63.1in
    Curb weight: 4,596lb

1973–1974 Thunderbird
    Wheelbase: 120.4in
    Overall length: 218.9in
    Overall width: 79.7in
    Front tread: 63in
    Rear tread: 63.1in
    Curb weight: 4,742lb

1975–1976 Thunderbird
    Wheelbase: 120.4in
    Overall length: 225.7in
    Height: 53.1in
    Overall width: 79.7in
    Front tread: 63in
    Rear tread: 63.1in
    Curb weight: 5,046–51,01lb

1977–1979 Thunderbird
    Wheelbase: 114in

Overall length 215.5in
Overall width: 78.5in
Height: 53in
Front tread: 63.2in
Rear tread: 63.1in
Curb Weight:
    Two-door hardtop: 4,028–4,122lb
    Town Landau with 400ci engine: 4,356lb

1980–1982 Thunderbird
    Wheelbase: 108.4in
    Overall length: 200.4in
    Height: 53.3in
    Width: 74.1in
    Front tread: 57in
    Rear tread: 58.1in
    Curb weight: 3,169–3,270lb

1983–1986 Thunderbird
    Wheelbase: 104in
    Overall length: 197.6in
    Front tread: 58.1in
    Rear tread: 58.5in
    Width: 71.1in
    Height: 53.2in
    Curb Weight:
        Thunderbird 3,073lb
        Turbo Coupe 3,172lb

1987–1988 Thunderbird
    Wheelbase: 104.2in
    Overall length: 202.1in
    Height: 53.4in
    Width: 71.1in
    Front tread: 58.1in
    Rear tread: 58.5in
    Curb weight: 3,133–3,380lb

1989–1993 Thunderbird
    Wheelbase: 113in
    Overall length: 198.7in
    Height: 52.7in
    Width: 72.7in
    Front tread: 61.6in
    Rear tread: 60.2in
    Curb weight: 3,550lb

Engines and Transmissions

1955 Thunderbird
  292ci Y-block V-8
  Bore and stroke: 3.75x3.3in
  Compression ratio:
    Manual transmission: 8.1:1
    Fordomatic: 8.5:1
  Carburetion: 4-barrel Holley
  Horsepower rating:
    Manual transmission: 193hp at 4400rpm
    Fordomatic: 198hp at 4400rpm
  Torque:
    Manual transmission: 280lb-ft at 2600rpm
    Fordomatic: 286lb-ft at 2500rpm
  Transmissions: three-speed manual,
    Fordomatic, AOD
  Rear axle ratios:
    Three-speed manual: 3.73:1
    Fordomatic: 3.31:1
    AOD: 3.92:1

1956 Thunderbird
  292ci Y-block V-8
  Bore and stroke: 3.75x3.30in
  Compression ratio: 8.4:1
  Carburetion: 4-barrel Holley
  Horsepower rating:
    Manual transmission: 200hp at 4600rpm
    Fordomatic: 202hp at 4600rpm
  Engine code: M

  312ci Y-block V-8
  Bore and stroke: 3.80x3.44in
  Compression ratio: 8.4.:1
  Carburetion: 4-barrel Holley
  Horsepower rating:
    Manual transmission 200hp at 4600rpm
    Fordomatic 202hp at 4600rpm
  Engine code: M

  312ci Y-block V-8
  Bore and stroke: 3.80x3.44in
  Compression ratio: 8.4:1
  Carburetion: 4-barrel Holley
  Horsepower:
    Manual transmission: 215hp at 4600rpm
    Fordomatic: 225hp at 4600rpm
  Engine code: P

1956 Thunderbird
  312ci Y-block V-8
  Bore and stroke: 3.80x3.44in
  Horsepower rating: 245hp at 4500rpm
  Torque: 332lb-ft at 3200rpm
  Compression ratio: 9.7:1
  Carburetion: 2x4-barrel Holleys
  Engine code: D
  Transmissions: three-speed manual, AOD,
    Fordomatic

1957 Thunderbird
  292ci Thunderbird V-8
  Bore and stroke: 3.75x3.30in
  Horsepower rating: 212hp at 4500rpm
  Torque: 297lb-ft at 2700rpm
  Transmission: three-speed manual
  Compression ratio: 9.1:1
  Carburetion: 2-barrel Ford or Holley
  Engine code: C
  312ci Thunderbird Special V-8
  Bore and stroke: 3.80x3.44in
  Horsepower rating: 245hp at 4500rpm
  Torque: 332lb-ft at 3200rpm
  Compression ratio: 9.7:1
  Carburetion: 4-barrel Holley
  Engine code: D
  Transmissions: AOD or Fordomatic

  312ci Thunderbird Super V-8
  Bore and stroke: 3.8x3.44in

Horsepower rating: 270hp at 4800rpm (285hp racing kit)
Torque: 336lb-ft at 3400rpm
Compression ratio: 9.7:1
Carburetion: 2x4-barrel Holley
Engine code: E
Transmissions: three-speed manual, AOD, Fordomatic
312ci Thunderbird supercharged V-8
Bore and stroke: 3.80x3.44in
Horsepower rating: 300hp at 4800rpm (340hp racing version)
Torque: 315lb-ft at 2600rpm
Compression ratio: 8.5:1
Carburetion: 4-barrel Holley
Supercharger: Paxton centrifugal-type
Transmissions: three-speed manual, AOD, Fordomatic

1958 Thunderbird
352ci Interceptor Special V-8
Bore and stroke: 4x3.5in
Horsepower rating: 300hp at 4600rpm
Compression ratio: 10.2:1
Carburetion: 4-barrel Holley
Torque : 381lb-ft at 2800rpm
Engine code: H
Transmissions: three-speed manual, AOD, Fordomatic

1959–1960 Thunderbird
352ci Thunderbird Special V-8
Bore and stroke: 4x3.5in
Compression ratio: 9.6:1
Carburetion: 4-barrel Holley 9510
Engine code:
    1959: H
    1960; Y
Horsepower rating: 300hp at 4600rpm
Torque: 381lb-ft at 2800rpm
Transmissions: three-speed manual, AOD, SelectShift Cruise-O-Matic

430ci Thunderbird Special V-8
Bore and stroke: 4.30x3.7in
Carburetion: 4-barrel Holley
Compression ratio: 10.0:1
Torque: 490lb-ft at 2800rpm
Engine code: J
Transmission: SelectShift Cruise-O-Matic

1961–1965 Thunderbird
390ci Thunderbird Special V-8
Bore and stroke: 4.05x3.78in
Carburetor: 4-barrel Holley
Engine code: Z
Horsepower rating: 300hp at 4600rpm

Torque: 427lb-ft at 2800rpm
Compression ratio: 9.6:1–10.1:1
Transmission: SelectShift Cruise-O-Matic

1962–1963 Thunderbird
390ci Thunderbird V-8
Bore and stroke: 4.05x3.78in
Carburetion: 3x2 Holleys
Engine code: M
Horsepower rating: 340hp at 5000rpm
Torque: 430lb-ft at 3200rpm
Compression ratio:
    1962: 10.5:1
    1963: 11.0:1
Transmission: SelectShift Cruise-O-Matic

1966–1968 Thunderbird
390ci Thunderbird V-8
Bore and stroke: 4.05x3.78in
Compression ratio: 10.5:1
Horsepower rating: 315hp at 4600rpm
Torque: 427lb-ft at 2800rpm
Engine code: Z
Transmission: SelectShift Cruise-O-Matic

428ci Thunderbird Special V-8
Bore and stroke: 4.13x3.98in
Compression ratio: 10.5:1
Horsepower rating: 345hp at 4600rpm (340hp in 1968)
Torque: 462lb-ft at 2800rpm
Engine code: Q
Transmission: SelectShift Cruise-O-Matic

1968–1971 Thunderbird
429ci Thunder-Jet V-8
Bore and Stroke: 4.36x3.59in
Horsepower rating: 360hp at 4600rpm
Torque: 476lb-ft at 2800rpm
Carburetor: 4-barrel Ford
Compression ratio: 10.5:1
Engine code: N
Transmission: SelectShift Cruise-O-Matic

1972–1973 Thunderbird
429ci Thunderbird V-8
Horsepower rating:
    1972: 212hp at 4400rpm
    1973: 208hp
Torque: 327lb-ft at 2600rpm
Compression ratio: 8.0:1
Carburetion: 4-barrel Motorcraft
Engine code: N
Transmission: SelectShift Cruise-O-Matic

460ci Thunderbird V-8
Bore and stroke: 4.36x3.85in

Horsepower rating:
  1972 224hp at 4400rpm
  1973 219hp
Torque: 342lb-ft at 2600rpm
Carburetor: 4-barrel Motorcraft
Engine code: A
Transmission: SelectShift Cruise-O-Matic

1974–1976 Thunderbird
  460ci Thunderbird V-8
  Bore and stroke: 4.36x3.85in
  Compression ratio: 8.0:1
  Horsepower rating: 220hp at 4000rpm
  Carburetor: 4-barrel Carter
  Engine code: A
  Transmission: SelectShift Cruise-O-Matic

1977–1979 Thunderbird
  302ci 2-barrel V-8
  351ci 2-barrel V-8
  400ci 2-barrel V-8
  Ford published no horsepower or torque
    specifications for its engines. The only
    transmission listed these years is an
    automatic.

1980 Thunderbird
  4.2-liter (255ci) 2-barrel V-8 (base engine)
  5.0-liter (302ci) 2-barrel V-8 (Optional)
  Transmissions:
    three-speed SelectShift
    Automatic (4.2-liter and 5.0-liter)
    AOD (Optional on 5.0-liter)

1981 Thunderbird
  3.3-liter (200ci) six 1-barrel Carb
  4.2-liter (255ci) V-8 2-barrel Carb
  5.0-liter (302ci) V-8 2-barrel Carb
  Transmissions:
    Three-speed SelectShift (3.3-liter and 4.2-
      liter)
    Four-speed AOD (standard on 5.0-liter,
      optional on 4.2-liter)

1982 Thunderbird
  3.3-liter (200ci) I-block six
  3.8-liter (232ci) V-6
  4.2-liter (255ci) 2-barrel V-8
  Transmissions:
    Three-speed SelectShift (3.3-liter)
    Four-speed AOD (standard on 4.2-liter and
      some 3.8-liter)

1983 Thunderbird
  3.8-liter (232ci) V-6 with EFI
  2.3-liter turbocharged four-cylinder (Turbo
    Coupe)

Transmissions:
  Three-speed SelectShift
  Four-speed AOD
  Five-speed manual (Turbo Coupe)

1984 Thunderbird
  3.8-liter (232ci) V-6 with EFI
  5.0-liter (302ci) V-8 with EFI
  2.3-liter (140ci) turbocharged four-cylinder
    (Turbo Coupe)
  Transmission:
    Three-speed SelectShift
    Four-speed AOD
    Five-speed manual (Turbo Coupe)

1985 Thunderbird
  2.3-liter (140ci) turbocharged four with EFI
    (Five-speed manual Turbo Coupe)
  2.3-liter (140ci) turbocharged four with EFI
    (Turbo Coupe with AOD)
  3.8-liter (232ci) V-6 with EFI three-speed
    SelectShift transmission
  3.8-liter (232ci) V-6 with EFI four-speed AOD
  5.0-liter (302ci) with EFI V-8 four-speed AOD

1986–1988 Thunderbird
  2.3-liter (140ci) turbocharged four with EFI
    (five-speed manual Turbo Coupe)
  2.3-liter (140ci) turbocharged four with EFI
    (four-speed AOD)
  3.8-liter (232ci) V-6 with EFI three-speed
    SelectShift transmission
  3.8-liter (232ci) with EFI V-6 four-speed AOD
  5.0-liter (302ci) with EFI V-8 four-speed AOD

1989–1990 Thunderbird:
  3.8-liter (232ci) with SEFI V-6
  3.8-liter (232ci) with SEFI supercharged V-6
  Transmission:
    Four-speed AOD
    Five-speed manual (standard on Super
      Coupe)
    Four-speed AOD (optional on Super
      Coupe)

1991–1993 Thunderbird
  3.8-liter (232ci) 140hp, 215lb-ft torque, with
    SEFI V-6
    Four-speed AOD
  3.8-liter (232ci) 210hp with SEFI V-6 super
    charged (Super Coupe)
  315lb-ft torque, five-speed manual or four-
    speed AOD
  5.0-liter (302ci)200hp at 4000rpm, 275lb-ft
    torque at 3000 rpm, V-8 with SEFI
  Four-speed AOD

Thunderbird Production Figures

1955: 16,155
1956: 15,631
1957: 21,380
1958: Hardtop-35,758
    Convertible-2134
1959: Hardtop-57,195
    Convertible-10,261
1960: Hardtop-78,447
    Convertible-11,860
    Sun Roof-2,536
1961: Hardtop-62,535
    Convertible-10,516
1962: Hardtop and Landau-68,127
    Convertible-8,457
    Sports Roadster-1,427
1963: Hardtop-42,806
    Convertible-5,913
    Landau-14,139
1964: Hardtop-60,552
    Landau-22,715
    Convertible-9,198
1965: Hardtop-42,652
    Landau-20,974
    Landau Special Edition-4500
    Convertible-6846
1966: Hardtop-13,389
    Town Hardtop-15,633
    Landau-35,105
    Convertible-5,049
1967: Hardtop-15,567
    Landau Two-door hardtop-37,442
    Landau Four-door-24,967
1968: Hardtop, bucket seats-5,420
    Landau Two-door, bucket seats-19,105
    Hardtop, bench seat-4,557
    Landau Two-door, bench seats-13,924
    Landau, Four-door, bucket seats-4,674
    Landau, Four-door, bench seat-17,251
1969: Hardtop, bucket seats-2361
    Hardtop, bench seat-3,552
    Landau, two-door, bucket seats-12,425
    Landau two-door, bench seat-15,239
    Landau four-door, bucket seats-1,983
    Landau four-door, bench seat-13,712
1970: Hardtop, bucket seats-1,925
    Hardtop, bench seat-3,191
    Landau two-door, bucket seats-16,953
    Landau two-door, bench seat-19,894
    Landau four-door, bucket seats-5,005
    Landau four-door, bench seat-3,396
1971: Hardtop, bucket seats-2,992
    Hardtop, bench seat-6,154
    Landau two-door, bucket seats-8,133
    Landau two-door, bench seat-12,223
    Landau four-door, bench seat-2,315
    Landau four-door, split-bench seat-4,238
1972: Hardtop-57,814
1973: Hardtop-87,269
1974: Hardtop-58,443
1975: Hardtop-42,685
1976: Hardtop-52,935
1977: Hardtop-318,140
1978: Hardtop-333,757
    Diamond Jubilee Edition-18,994
1979: Hardtop-284,141
1980: Hardtop-156,803
1981: Coupe-86,693
1982: Coupe-45,142
1983: Coupe-121,999
1984: Coupe-170,533
1985: Coupe-151,851
1986: Coupe-163,965
1987: Coupe-128,135
1988: Coupe-147,243
1989: Coupe-101,906
    Super Coupe-12,962
1990: Coupe-90,247
    Super Coupe-20,339
    Thirty-fifth Anniversary Edition-3,371
1991: Coupe-75,547
    Super Coupe-7,267
1992: Coupe-73,175
    Super Coupe-4,614
1993: LX and Super Coupe-122,415

Parts and
Services Sources

Alabama
Thunderbirds USA
3621 Resource Drive
Tuscaloosa, AL 35401
800-842-5557
1955–1957 Parts and Accessories

Arizona
T-Bird Connection
728 East Dunlap
Phoenix, AZ 85020
602-997-9285
1958–1972 Thunderbird parts

California
Don Simpkin
14006 Paramount
Paramount, CA 90723
New and used parts 1955–1966

Convertible Service
5126 H Walnut Grove Avenue
San Gabriel, CA 91776
818-285-2255
Convertible parts

Automotive Information
Box 1746
La Mesa, CA 91944
Shop manuals

Larry's Mustang and Thunderbird Parts
511 South Raymond Avenue
Fullerton, CA 92631
714-871-6432
1955–1966 Thunderbird parts

Thunderbird Headquarters
1080 Detroit Avenue
Concord, CA 94518
510-825-9550
1955–1956 Thunderbird parts

Concours Parts
3563 Numancia Street
Santa, Ynez, CA 93460
805-688-7795
1955–1957 Thunderbird parts

Prestige Thunderbirds, Inc.
10215 Greenleaf Avenue
Santa Fe Springs, CA 90670
800-423-4751
1955–1957 Thunderbird parts

Nick's T-Birds
20928 Osborne Street H
Canoga Park, CA 91304
818-700-8383

Exhaust systems for 1955–1974 Thunderbirds
Classic Thunderbird Parts
1048 West Collins Avenue
Orange, CA 92667
1955–1966 Thunderbird Parts

National Parts Depot
1376 Walter Street #1
Ventura, CA 93003
(805) 654-0468
800-235-3445
1955–1957 Thunderbird parts

Colorado
The Body Shop
732 South Wahsatch
Colorado Springs, CO 80903
(719) 633-1211
1955–1957 Thunderbird restorations

Florida
National Parts Depot
3101 Southwest 40th Boulevard
Gainesville, FL 32608
800-874-7595
1955–1957 Thunderbird parts

Bob's T-Birds
5397 Northeast 14th Avenue
Fort Lauderdale, FL 33334
305-491-6652
Complete restoration services

T-Bird Restorations
363 Ansin Boulevard
Hallandale, FL 33009
1955–1966 Thunderbird restorations

Idaho
Classic Auto Parts
2945-1/2 Government Way
Coeur d'Alene, ID 83814
206-667-3428
Parting out 1961–1975 Thunderbirds

Maryland
Quality Thunderbird Parts
701 Old Crossing Drive
Baltimore, MD 21208
410-653-9595
1964–1966 parts and accessories

Massachusetts
David Edwards
Box 245 HT
Needham, MA 02194
Fordomatic rebuild kits

Hydro-E-Lectric
48 Appleton
Auburn, MA 01501
508-832-3081
Convertible parts

Michigan
Thunderbird Center
23610 John R
Hazel Park, MI 48030
313-548-3033
1955–1957 new and used parts

Lois Eminger
Box 220
Dearborn, MI 48121-0220
Original Thunderbird window stickers

Classic Suspension
6000 Williams Lake Road
Waterford, MI 48329
313-623-0885
Leaf-spring manufacturers

Radio and Wheelcover World
2718 Koper
Sterling Heights, MI 48310
313-977-7979
1955–1992 Thunderbird radios

Original Auto Interiors
7869 Trumble Road
Columbus, MI 48063
313-727-2486
1958–1966 Thunderbird interiors

Minnesota
Class Tech
1400 Arboretum Boulevard
Victoria, MN 55386
800-874-9981
1955–1957 Thunderbird wiring looms

Mississippi
Classique Cars Unlimited
5 Turkey Bayou Road
Lakeshore, MS 39558
601-467-9633
1958–1988 Thunderbird parts

Missouri
Kansas City Thunderbird
5002 Gardner
Kansas City, MO 64120
1958–1969 Thunderbird used parts

Nebraska
Nebraska Ford Parts
1845 South 48th
Lincoln, NE 68506
402-489-3036
NOS Thunderbird parts

Auto Kraft
712 West Cornhusker Highway
Lincoln, Nebraska 68521
402-474-2344
SWB Thunderbird Super Coupe

New Jersey
Kanter Auto Products
76 Monroe Street
Boonton, NJ 07005
201-334-9575
Shop manuals, parts

New Mexico
Victor Yarberry
6831 Truchas Drive Northeast
Albuquerque, NM 87109
505-821-1002 (after 6:00 pm MST)
1965–1971 Electronic turn signal sequencers

New York
Muck Motors
10 Campbell Boulevard
Buffalo, NY 14068-1299
716-688-5464
1958–1966 Thunderbird parts and trim

Thunderbird Parts and Restoration
5844 Goodrich Road
Clarence Center, NY 14032

716-741-2866
1958–1968 Thunderbird parts and accessories

Custom Autocraft
Flowerfield Building #2
St. James, NY 11780
516-862-7469
1955–1957 Thunderbird reproduction steel body parts

North Carolina
Dennis Carpenter Reproductions
P.O. Box 26398
Charlotte, NC 28221
704-786-8139
1955–1966 Thunderbird parts

Classic Body
4010 A Hartley Street
Charlotte, NC 28206
704-596-5186
1955–1971 Thunderbird sheet metal

Bob Walker's Thunderbirds
P.O. Box 1091
Gastonia, NC 28053-1091
704-867-5557
1955–1957 Thunderbird parts

Ohio
Classic Auto Supply
795 High Street
Coshocton, OH 43812
614-622-8561
1955–1957 parts and restoration services

Hill's Classic Cars Restoration
29670 Bashan Road
Racine, OH 45771
(614) 949-2217
1955–1957 Thunderbird restorations

Oregon
Dick Martin's Bird Nest
745 Southeast 9th
Portland, OR 97214
503-231-6669
1958–1966 Thunderbird parts

The T-Bird Sanctuary
7849 Southwest Cirrus Drive #24
Beaverton, OR 97005
503-641-0556
1958-1976 Thunderbird parts

Jerry Bougher
3628 Union Street Southeast

Albany, OR 97321
(503) 928-6919
Magazine advertisements

Pennsylvania
Thunderbirds East
Box 207
Lenni, PA 19052
215-358-1021
1955–1957 Thunderbird new and used parts

The Bird's Nest
RD 1 Box 1430
Deer Lake, PA 17961
717-366-1644
Restoration services

Bob's Bird House
124 Watkins Avenue
Chadds Ford, PA 19317
215-358-3420
1958–1976 parts, cars, service

Tom Sestak
4529 Meadow Drive
Nazareth, PA 18064
1955–1957 Thunderbird parts

Texas
T-Bird Nest
2550 East Southlake Boulevard
Southlake, TX 76092
817-481-1776
1958–1966 parts, repairs, restorations

Dennis Classic Thunderbird Shop
301 Cavalier
Pasadena, TX
713-947-BIRD
1955–1957 new and used parts

Amos Minter
17730 Davenport Road North
Dallas, TX 75252
214-931-3357
Buying, selling, restoring 1955–1957 Thunderbirds

Wisconsin
Peter Zierden
9161 South 46th Street
Franklin, WI 53132
414-764-6630
Thunderbird exhaust system parts

Jeff VanderZanden
414-498-8345
1955–1957 Thunderbird Jr. reproductions

Additional Reading

If you like reading books about the Ford Thunderbird, you might want to add the following titles to your library. Each one has a lot to offer the Thunderbird enthusiast.

Boyer, William P. *Thunderbird: An Odyssey in Automotive Design*. Taylor Publishing, 1986.

William P. Boyer is a retired Ford designer who worked on the Thunderbird from the earliest days. This book covers the history of the Thunderbird from an insider's point of view. There are plenty of photographs that show how the Thunderbird evolved over the years. This book covers Thunderbirds through 1985.

Miller, Ray. *Thunderbird: An Illustrated History of the Ford Thunderbird*. The Evergreen Press, 1973.

Covers Thunderbirds from 1955 through 1966 in a photographic collection. Some of the photographs are quite detailed and show the differences between Thunderbirds.

Katz, John. *Soaring Spirit: Thirty-five Years of the Ford Thunderbird*. Automobile Quarterly, 1989.

Covers the Thunderbird from 1955 through 1990. Lots of photographs and text to describe how the Thunderbird developed through the years.

Clubs and Organizations

The Classic Thunderbird Club International Inc.
11823 East Slauson Avenue Unit #39
Santa Fe Springs, CA 90670-1148

The Classic Thunderbird Club International was incorporated in 1964, and covers all Thunderbirds built from 1955 through 1957. In the United States, regions and local chapters promote meets and shows on a national, as well as regional, basis. The club also reproduces parts and literature for members. Its *Early Bird* magazine is full of interesting articles about these fine cars and their owners.

Vintage Thunderbird Club International
P.O. Box 2250
Dearborn, MI 48123-2250

The Vintage Thunderbird Club International covers all Thunderbirds produced between 1958 and 1967. Through its member chapters, the club promotes regional and national shows and conventions that bring 1958–1966 Thunderbird enthusiasts together. This club also offers technical advice as well as a concours rulebook to help members restore their cars or add the detailing necessary to make them look their best. Its *Thunderbird Scoop* magazine is full of information.

Index